Programming Entity Framework:
Code First

Julia Lerman and Rowan Miller

O'REILLY®

Beijing · Cambridge · Farnham · Köln · Sebastopol · Tokyo

Programming Entity Framework: Code First
by Julia Lerman and Rowan Miller

Copyright © 2012 Julia Lerman, Rowan Miller. All rights reserved.
Printed in the United States of America.

Published by O'Reilly Media, Inc., 1005 Gravenstein Highway North, Sebastopol, CA 95472.

O'Reilly books may be purchased for educational, business, or sales promotional use. Online editions are also available for most titles (*http://my.safaribooksonline.com*). For more information, contact our corporate/institutional sales department: (800) 998-9938 or *corporate@oreilly.com*.

Editor: Meghan Blanchette	**Cover Designer:** Karen Montgomery
Production Editor: Teresa Elsey	**Interior Designer:** David Futato
	Illustrator: Robert Romano

Revision History for the First Edition:
　　2011-11-18　　First release
See *http://oreilly.com/catalog/errata.csp?isbn=9781449312947* for release details.

ISBN: 978-1-449-31294-7

[LSI]

1321545516

Table of Contents

Preface

Microsoft's principal data access technology, ADO.NET Entity Framework, has had two major releases as part of the .NET Framework. NET 3.5 brought us the first version of Entity Framework, which is covered in the first edition of *Programming Entity Framework*. In 2010, Microsoft .NET 4 was released; it contained the next version of Entity Framework, referred to as Entity Framework 4. The completely revised second edition of *Programming Entity Framework* was dedicated to teaching readers how to use this version of Entity Framework in Visual Studio 2010.

When .NET 4 was released, the Entity Framework team was already hard at work on a new addition, called Code First, to provide an alternative to building the Entity Data Model that is core to Entity Framework. Rather than using a visual designer, Code First allows you to create the model from your existing classes.

This book is dedicated to teaching readers how to use Code First to build and configure a model based on the classes in your business domain. While Code First can do much of the job of inferring a model from your classes, there is quite a lot that you can do to affect the model that Code First creates.

In this book, you will learn what Code First does by default (aka convention) and how to perform further configuration to affect how it understands your properties, classes, relationships, and the database schema they map to—whether you use Code First to help create a database or you want to use it with an existing database. With this knowledge, you can reap the benefits of the Entity Framework while leveraging existing classes or those classes you might be building for a new software project.

Audience

This book is designed for .NET developers who have experience with Visual Studio and database management basics. Prior experience with Entity Framework is beneficial but not required. The code samples in this book are written in C#, with some of these samples also expressed in Visual Basic. There are a number of online tools that you can use to convert snippets of C# into Visual Basic.

Contents of This Book

This book contains eight chapters.

Chapter 1

> This chapter provides a high level, end-to-end overview of Code First. You'll find sample code, but there are no walkthroughs in this first chapter. The chapter winds up with a discussion of what you won't find in Code First, so that you can approach the technology with the correct expectations.

Chapter 2

> In this chapter, you will get to jump right in to the code. The chapter gives you a chance to work hands-on with Code First (or just read along if you prefer) as you work with a simple class to see some of the basic default behavior and perform some simple configurations using the two mechanisms for configuring: Data Annotations and the Fluent API. You'll see how Code First is able to automatically create a database for you using default behavior. Through the next four chapters you'll lean on this database creation default, and then in Chapter 6, you'll learn how to work with existing databases and exert more control over the database.

Chapter 3

> This is the first of three chapters that dive deeply into Code First convention and configuration. You'll learn about the presumptions the Code First convention makes about the attributes of properties (e.g., the length of strings) and how that gets interpreted into the conceptual model and the database. You'll also learn how to perform configuration using Data Annotations and Fluent API to control the outcome of the model and database.

Chapter 4

> In this chapter, you'll focus on relationships between your classes and how those work out in the model that Code First infers and in the database. Code First convention is able to infer the most common scenarios when classes have relationships between them. We'll look closely at the nuances in your classes that will drive Code First's assumptions and then how to ensure that Code First knows exactly what you want it to do, again by configuring with Data Annotations or the Fluent API.

Chapter 5

> This chapter focuses on how classes map to the database. This information will be especially important when you are mapping your classes to an existing database. Simple mappings, such as specifying table names or column names and types, can make a huge difference. You'll learn about the default mappings to the database when you have inheritance hierarchies defined between your classes and how to drive Table Per Hierarchy, Table Per Type and even Table Per Concrete Type

mappings to the database. You'll also learn how to map a single entity to multiple tables or, conversely, multiple entities to a single table.

Chapter 6

This chapter is where you finally get to stray from the default database creation behavior. You'll learn how to control Code First's determination of the database name and location, whether you do this through connection strings or some lower-level code in the Code First API. You'll also find some additional tricks for controlling connections and more.

Chapter 7

In this chapter, you'll dig farther into Code First to see how to perform some advanced techniques. You'll see how to prevent Code First from worrying about keeping the database in sync with your model when you want to take over control of that task. You'll also learn about the default model caching and how to override it to solve problems like targeting multiple database providers in the same application instance. Other advanced topics are addressed as well.

Chapter 8

This book was written about the features of Code First based on the Entity Framework 4.2 release. At the time of this writing, a number of Community Technical Previews demonstrate some of the features that Code First will gain in upcoming releases. This chapter shares available information about these future releases.

Conventions Used in This Book

The following typographical conventions are used in this book:

Italic
: Indicates new terms, URLs, email addresses, filenames, and file extensions.

`Constant width`
: Used for program listings, as well as within paragraphs to refer to program elements such as variable or function names, databases, data types, environment variables, statements, and keywords.

`Constant width bold`
: Shows commands or other text that should be typed literally by the user.

`Constant width italic`
: Shows text that should be replaced with user-supplied values or by values determined by context.

This icon signifies a tip, suggestion, or general note.

This icon indicates a warning or caution.

Using Code Examples

This book is here to help you get your job done. In general, you may use the code in this book in your programs and documentation. You do not need to contact us for permission unless you're reproducing a significant portion of the code. For example, writing a program that uses several chunks of code from this book does not require permission. Selling or distributing a CD-ROM of examples from O'Reilly books does require permission. Answering a question by citing this book and quoting example code does not require permission. Incorporating a significant amount of example code from this book into your product's documentation does require permission.

We appreciate, but do not require, attribution. An attribution usually includes the title, author, publisher, and ISBN. For example: "*Programming Entity Framework: Code First* by Julia Lerman and Rowan Miller (O'Reilly). Copyright 2012 Julia Lerman, Rowan Miller, 978-1-449-31294-7."

If you feel your use of code examples falls outside fair use or the permission given above, feel free to contact us at *permissions@oreilly.com*.

Safari® Books Online

Safari Books Online is an on-demand digital library that lets you easily search over 7,500 technology and creative reference books and videos to find the answers you need quickly.

With a subscription, you can read any page and watch any video from our library online. Read books on your cell phone and mobile devices. Access new titles before they are available for print, and get exclusive access to manuscripts in development and post feedback for the authors. Copy and paste code samples, organize your favorites, download chapters, bookmark key sections, create notes, print out pages, and benefit from tons of other time-saving features.

O'Reilly Media has uploaded this book to the Safari Books Online service. To have full digital access to this book and others on similar topics from O'Reilly and other publishers, sign up for free at *http://my.safaribooksonline.com*.

How to Contact Us

Please address comments and questions concerning this book to the publisher:

O'Reilly Media, Inc.
1005 Gravenstein Highway North
Sebastopol, CA 95472
800-998-9938 (in the United States or Canada)
707-829-0515 (international or local)
707-829-0104 (fax)

We have a web page for this book, where we list errata, examples, and any additional information. You can access this page at:

http://shop.oreilly.com/product/0636920022220.do

To comment or ask technical questions about this book, send email to:

bookquestions@oreilly.com

For more information about our books, courses, conferences, and news, see our website at *http://www.oreilly.com*.

Find us on Facebook: *http://facebook.com/oreilly*

Follow us on Twitter: *http://twitter.com/oreillymedia*

Watch us on YouTube: *http://www.youtube.com/oreillymedia*

Acknowledgments

Special thanks to technical reviewers Andrew Peters, from the Entity Framework team, and Suzanne Shushereba, a software developer at Fletcher Allen Health Care in Burlington, Vermont (and a friend). Andrew leveraged his expertise in Code First to ensure that we hadn't made any technical gaffes. Suzanne was new to Code First but not Entity Framework. She not only read the text to point out where we could provide a better explanation for a newbie, but she also followed along with the walkthroughs in Visual Studio to help us find places where providing additional code would be more helpful.

Thanks to Microsoft for making it easy for Rowan to participate in this project.

Thanks once again to O'Reilly Media for providing their support.

CHAPTER 1

Welcome to Code First

Microsoft's ADO.NET Entity Framework, known widely as EF, introduced out-of-the-box Object Relational Mapping to .NET and Visual Studio. Central to Entity Framework was the Entity Data Model, a conceptual model of your application domain that maps back to the schema of your database. This conceptual model describes the core classes in your application. Entity Framework uses this conceptual model while querying from the database, creating objects from that data and then persisting changes back to the database.

Modeling with EF Before Code First

The first iteration of Entity Framework, which came as part of .NET 3.5 and Visual Studio 2008, gave developers the ability to create this conceptual model by reverse engineering an existing database into an XML file. This XML file used the EDMX extension, and you could use a designer to view and customize the model to better suit your domain. Visual Studio 2010 and .NET 4 brought the second version of Entity Framework, named Entity Framework 4 (EF4), to align with the .NET version. On the modeling side, a new capability called Model First was added. Here you could design your conceptual model in the visual designer and then create the database based on the model.

Model First allows developers working on new projects that do not have legacy databases to benefit from the Entity Framework as well. Developers can start with a focus on their application domain by designing the conceptual model and let the database creation flow from that process.

Whether designing the EDMX by the database-first or model-first way, the next step for creating your domain is to let automatic code generation build classes based on the entities and their relationships that it finds in the model. From here, developers have strongly typed classes representing their domain objects—whether those are customers, baseball cards, or fairy-tale characters—and can go on their merry way developing their software applications around these classes.

Another critical change came in EF4. In .NET 3.5, the only way Entity Framework was able to manage in-memory objects was by requiring classes to inherit from Entity Framework's `EntityObject`. The `EntityObject` communicates its changes to Entity Framework, which in turns keeps track of changes and eventually is able to persist them back to the database. In addition to this functionality, .NET 4 introduced POCO (Plain Old CLR Object) support to enable the Entity Framework to track changes to simpler classes without needing the `EntityObject` to be involved. This freed up developers to use their own classes, independent of Entity Framework. The EF runtime had a way of being aware of the classes and keeping track of them while in memory.

Inception of Code First

Building upon the pieces that were introduced in EF4, Microsoft was able to create one more path to modeling, which many developers have been requesting since EF's inception. This new type of modeling is called Code First. Code First lets you define your domain model with code rather than using an XML-based EDMX file. Even though Model First and Database First use code generation to provide classes for you to work with, many developers simply did not want to work with a designer nor have their classes generated for them. They just wanted to write code.

In Code First you begin by defining your domain model using POCO classes, which have no dependency on Entity Framework. Code First can infer a lot of information about your model purely from the shape of your classes. You can also provide additional configuration to further describe your model or override what Code First inferred. This configuration is also defined in code: no XML files or designers.

 EF4 also has support for POCO classes when working with the designer. The EF team provided a POCO template that would allow POCO classes to be generated for you. These generated classes would be automatically updated as you made changes in the designer. You could also use your own POCO classes rather than having them generated for you. But if you decided to take this approach, you were responsible for keeping your classes and the EDMX file in sync. This meant that any changes had to be made in two places—once in the designer and again in your classes. One of the big advantages of Code First is that your classes become the model. This means any changes to the model only need to be made in one place—your POCO classes.

Code First, Database First, and Model First are all just ways of building an Entity Data Model that can be used with Entity Framework to perform data access. Once the model has been built, the Entity Framework runtime behaves the same, regardless of how you created the model. Whether you choose to go with a designer or to use the code-based modeling is entirely your decision. Figure 1-1 lays out the different options you have for modeling with Entity Framework.

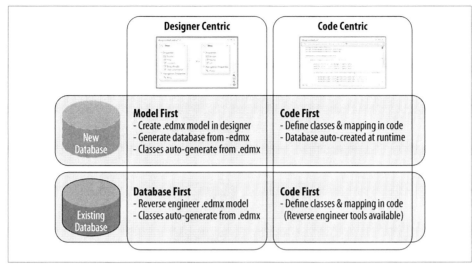

Figure 1-1. Modeling workflow options

Microsoft refers to the Database First, Model First, and Code First options as *workflows* (e.g., the Code First workflow). That's because each of those options is really a set of steps, whether you execute the steps yourself or the steps happen automatically. For example, with the Database First workflow, you reverse engineer from a database and then let a code generator create the classes. The Code First workflow begins with you coding your classes and then optionally letting Code First create a database for you.

Getting Code First to Developers in Between .NET Releases

Code First was not ready in time to be released in .NET 4. Rather than waiting for the .NET 5 release to bring Code First to developers, Microsoft made Code First available in an out-of-band release, referred to as Entity Framework 4.1, in April 2011. The version number will increment as subsequent updates are released. Entity Framework 4.2 was released in October 2011 and replaces Entity Framework 4.1 as the release that included Code First. The core Entity Framework API, *System.Data.Entity.dll*, is still part of the .NET Framework and was untouched by Entity Framework 4.1 and 4.2.

The Entity Framework 4.1 release also included another important feature, called the DbContext API. DbContext is the core of this API, which also contains other dependent classes. DbContext is a lighter-weight version of the Entity Framework's ObjectContext. It is a wrapper over ObjectContext, and it exposes only those features that Microsoft found were most commonly used by developers working with Entity Framework. The DbContext also provides simpler access to coding patterns that are more complex to achieve with the `ObjectContext`. `DbContext` also takes care of a lot of common tasks for you, so that you write less code to achieve the same tasks; this is particularly true when working with Code First. Because Microsoft recommends that you use `DbContext` with Code First, you will see it used throughout this book. However, a separate book, called *Programming Entity Framework: DbContext*, will delve more deeply into `DbContext`, `DbSet`, Validation API, and other features that arrived alongside the `DbContext`.

Figure 1-2 helps you to visualize how Code First and DbContext add functionality by building on the core Entity Framework 4 API, rather than modifying it.

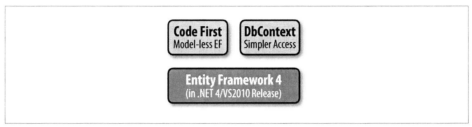

Figure 1-2. Code First and DbContext built on EF4

Flexible Release Schedule

Microsoft will continue to release new features on top of Entity Framework using Visual Studio's Library Package Management distribution (aka NuGet) mechanism that is used for Entity Framework 4.2. The core EF libraries that are in .NET will evolve with .NET releases. But features such as Code First and DbContext that rely on the core will be distributed when they are ready by way of updates to the Entity Framework NuGet package.

Writing the Code...First

Code First is aptly named: the code comes first, the rest follows. Let's take a look at the basic default functionality without worrying about all of the possible scenarios you might need to support. The rest of the book is dedicated to that.

 We don't expect you to recreate the sample code shown in this first chapter. The code samples are presented as part of an overview, not as a walkthrough. Beginning with Chapter 2, you will find many walkthroughs. They are described in a way that you can follow along in Visual Studio and try things out yourself if you'd like.

Of course, the first thing you'll need is some code—classes to describe a business domain. In this case a very small one, patients and patient visits for a veterinarian.

Example 1-1 displays three classes for this domain—Patient, Visit, and AnimalType.

Example 1-1. Domain classes

```
using System;
using System.Collections.Generic;

namespace ChapterOneProject
{
  class Patient
  {
    public Patient()
    {
      Visits = new List<Visit>();
    }
    public int Id { get; set; }
    public string Name { get; set; }
    public DateTime BirthDate { get; set; }
    public AnimalType AnimalType { get; set; }
    public DateTime FirstVisit { get; set; }
    public List<Visit> Visits { get; set; }
  }

  class Visit
  {
    public int Id { get; set; }
    public DateTime Date { get; set; }
    public String ReasonForVisit { get; set; }
    public String Outcome { get; set; }
    public Decimal Weight { get; set; }
    public int PatientId { get; set; }
  }

  class AnimalType
  {
    public int Id { get; set; }
    public string TypeName { get; set; }
  }
}
```

Core to Code First is the concept of conventions—default rules that Code First will use to build a model based on your classes. For example, Entity Framework requires that a class that it will manage has a key property. Code First has a convention that if it finds a property named Id or a property with the combined name of the type name and Id (e.g., PatientId), that property will be automatically configured as the key. If it can't find a property that matches this convention, it will throw an exception at runtime telling you that there is no key. Other types of conventions determine the default length of a string, or the default table structure that Entity Framework should expect in the database when you have classes that inherit from each other.

This could be very limiting if Code First relied solely on convention to work with your classes. But Code First is not determined to force you to design your classes to meet its needs. Instead, the conventions exist to enable Code First to automatically handle some common scenarios. If your classes happen to follow convention, Code First doesn't need any more information from you. Entity Framework will be able to work directly with your classes. If they don't follow convention, you can provide additional information through Code First's many configuration options to ensure that your classes are interpreted properly by Code First.

In the case of the three classes in Example 1-1, the Id properties in each class meet the convention for keys. We'll let Code First work with these classes as they are without any additional configurations.

Managing Objects with DbContext

The domain classes described above have nothing to do with the Entity Framework. They have no knowledge of it. That's the beauty of working with Code First. You get to use your own classes. This is especially beneficial if you have existing domain classes from another project.

To use Code First, you start by defining a class that inherits from DbContext. One of the roles of this class, which we'll refer to as a context, is to let Code First know about the classes that make up your model. That's how Entity Framework will be aware of them and be able to keep track of them. This is done by exposing the domain classes through another new class introduced along with DbContext—the DbSet. Just as DbContext is a simpler wrapper around the ObjectContext, DbSet is a wrapper around Entity Framework 4's ObjectSet, which simplifies coding tasks for which we normally use the ObjectSet.

Example 1-2 shows what this context class might look like. Notice that there are DbSet properties for Patients and Visits. The DbSets will allow you to query against the types. But we don't anticipate doing a direct query of AnimalTypes, so there's no need for a DbSet of AnimalTypes. Code First is smart enough to know that Patient makes use of the AnimalType class and will therefore include it in the model.

Example 1-2. VetContext class which derives from DbContext

```
using System.Data.Entity;

namespace ChapterOneProject
{
  class VetContext:DbContext
  {
    public DbSet<Patient> Patients { get; set; }
    public DbSet<Visit> Visits { get; set; }
  }
}
```

Using the Data Layer and Domain Classes

Now here comes what may seem a little surprising. This is all you need for a data layer—that is based on the assumption that you're going to rely 100 percent on Code First convention to do the rest of the work.

There's no database connection string. There is not even a database yet. But still, you are ready to use this data layer. Example 1-3 shows a method that will create a new dog `PatientType` along with our first `Patient`. The method also creates the `Patient`'s first `Visit` record and adds it to the `Patient.Visits` property.

Then we instantiate the context, add the patient to the `DbSet<Patient>` (`Patients`) that is defined in the context, and finally call `SaveChanges`, which is a method of `DbContext`.

Example 1-3. Adding a patient to the database with the VetContext

```
private static void CreateNewPatient()
{
  var dog = new AnimalType { TypeName = "Dog" };
  var patient = new Patient
  {
    Name = "Sampson",
    BirthDate = new DateTime(2008, 1, 28),
    AnimalType = dog,
    Visits = new List<Visit>
    {
      new Visit
      {
       Date = new DateTime(2011, 9, 1)
      }
    }
  };

  using(var context = new VetContext())
  {
    context.Patients.Add(patient);
    context.SaveChanges();
  }
}
```

Remember that there's no connection string anywhere and no known database. Yet after running this code, we can look in the local SQL Server Express instance and see a new database whose name matches the fully qualified name of the context class, `ChapterOneProject.VetContext`.

You can see the details of this database's schema in Figure 1-3.

Compare the database schema to the classes defined in Example 1-1. They match almost exactly, table to class and field to property. The only difference is that a foreign key, `Patients.AnimalType_Id`, was created, even though there was no foreign key property in the `Patient` class. Code First worked out that because of the relationship expressed in the class (`Patient` has a reference to `AnimalType`), a foreign key would be

```
ChapterOneProject.VetContext
  Tables
    System Tables
    dbo.AnimalTypes
      Columns
        Id (PK, int, not null)
        TypeName (nvarchar(max), null)
    dbo.Patients
      Columns
        Id (PK, int, not null)
        Name (nvarchar(max), null)
        BirthDate (datetime, not null)
        AnimalType_Id (FK, int, null)
    dbo.Visits
      Columns
        Id (PK, int, not null)
        Date (datetime, not null)
        ReasonForVisit (nvarchar(max), null)
        Outcome (nvarchar(max), null)
        Weight (decimal(18,2), not null)
        PatientId (FK, int, not null)
```

Figure 1-3. The new database created by Code First

needed in the database to persist that relationship. This is one of many conventions that Code First uses when it's dealing with relationships. There are many ways to express relationships between classes. Code First conventions are able to interpret many of them. Notice, for example, that the `PatientId` field, which has an explicit property in the `Visit` class, is not null, whereas the `AnimalType_Id` field that Code First inferred from a navigation property is nullable. Again, convention determined the nullability of the foreign keys, but if you want to modify how Code First interprets your classes, you can do so using additional configuration.

Getting from Classes to a Database

If you have worked with Entity Framework, you are familiar with the model that is expressed in an EDMX file that you work with in a visual designer. You may also be aware of the fact that the EDMX file is in fact an XML file, but the designer makes it much easier to work with. The XML used to describe the model has a very specific schema and working with the raw XML would be mind-boggling without the designer.

What is not as obvious in the designer is that the XML contains more than just the description of the conceptual model that is displayed in the designer. It also has a description of database schema that the classes map to and one last bit of XML that describes how to get from the classes and properties to the tables and columns in the database. The combination of the model XML, the database schema XML, and the mapping XML are referred to as *metadata*.

At runtime, the Entity Framework reads the XML that describes all three parts of the XML and creates an in-memory representation of the metadata. But the in-memory metadata is not the XML; it is strongly typed objects such as `EntityType`, `EdmProperty`, and `AssociationType`. Entity Framework interacts with this in-memory representation of the model and schema every time it needs to interact with the database.

Because there is no XML file with Code First, it creates the in-memory metadata from what it can discover in your domain classes. This is where convention and configuration come into play. Code First has a class called the `DbModelBuilder`. It is the `DbModelBuilder` that reads the classes and builds the in-memory model to the best of its ability. Since it is also building the portion of the metadata that represents the database schema, it is able to use that to create the database. If you add configurations to help the model builder determine what the model and database schema should look like, it will read those just after it inspects the classes and incorporate that information into its understanding of what the model and database schema should look like.

Figure 1-4 shows how Entity Framework can build the in-memory model from code or from an XML file maintained through the designer. Once the in-memory model is created, Entity Framework doesn't need to know how the model was created. It can use the in-memory model to determine what the database schema should look like, build queries to access data, translate the results of queries into your objects, and persist changes to those objects back to the database.

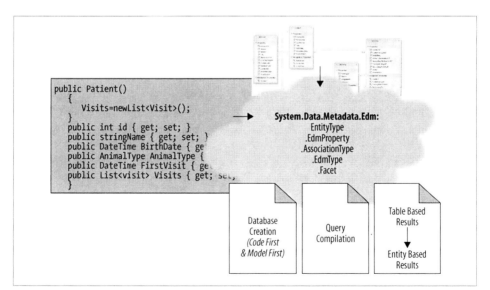

Figure 1-4. In-memory metadata created from code or EDMX model

Working with Configuration

In those cases where Code First needs some help understanding your intent, you have two options for performing configuration: Data Annotations and Code First's Fluent API. Which option you choose is most often based on personal preference and your coding style. There is some advanced configuration that is only possible via the Fluent API.

Code First allows you to configure a great variety of property attributes, relationships, inheritance hierarchies, and database mappings. You'll get a sneak peek at configuration now, but the bulk of this book is dedicated to explaining the convention and configuration options that are available to you.

Configuring with Data Annotations

One way to apply configuration, which many developers like because it is so simple, is to use Data Annotations. Data Annotations are attributes that you apply directly to the class or properties that you want to affect. These can be found in the System.Component Model.DataAnnotations namespace.

For example, if you want to ensure that a property should always have a value, you can use the Required annotation. In Example 1-4, this annotation has been applied to the AnimalType's TypeName property.

Example 1-4. Using an annotation to mark a property as required

```
class AnimalType
{
  public int Id { get; set; }
  [Required]
  public string TypeName { get; set; }
}
```

This will have two effects. The first is that the TypeName field in the database will become not null. The second is that it will be validated by Entity Framework, thanks to the Validation API that was also introduced in Entity Framework 4.1. By default, when it's time to SaveChanges, Entity Framework will check to be sure that the property you have flagged as Required is not empty. If it is empty, Entity Framework will throw an exception.

The Required annotation affects the database column facets and property validation. Some annotations are specific only to database mappings. For example, the Table annotation tells Code First that the class maps to a table of a certain name. The data that you refer to as AnimalType in your application might be stored in a table called Spe cies. The Table annotation allows you to specify this mapping.

Example 1-5. Specifying a table name to map to

```
[Table("Species")]
class AnimalType
{
  public int Id { get; set; }
  [Required]
  public string TypeName { get; set; }
}
```

Configuring with the Fluent API

While applying configurations with Data Annotations is quite simple to do, specifying metadata within a domain class may not align with your style of development. There is an alternative way to add configurations that uses Code First's Fluent API. With configuration applied via the Fluent API, your domain classes remain "clean." Rather than modify the classes, you provide the configuration information to Code First's model builder in a method exposed by the DbContext. The method is called OnModel Creating. Example 1-6 demonstrates the same configurations that were used above, but now applied using the Fluent API. In each configuration, the code specifies that the model builder should configure the AnimalType.

Example 1-6. Configuring the model using the Fluent API

```
class VetContext:DbContext
{
  public DbSet<Patient> Patients { get; set; }
  public DbSet<Visit> Visits { get; set; }

  protected override void OnModelCreating
   (DbModelBuilder modelBuilder)
  {
    modelBuilder.Entity<AnimalType>()
              .ToTable("Species");
    modelBuilder.Entity<AnimalType>()
              .Property(p => p.TypeName).IsRequired();
  }
}
```

The first configuration uses the Fluent API equivalent of the Table Data Annotation, which is the ToTable method, and passes in the name of the table to which the Animal Type class should be mapped. The second configuration uses a lambda expression to identify one of the properties of AnimalType and then appends the IsRequired method to that property.

This is just one way to build fluent configurations. You will learn much more about using both Data Annotations and the Fluent API to configure property attributes, relationships, inheritance hierarchies, and database mappings in the following chapters.

Creating or Pointing to a Database

Earlier in this chapter, you saw that by default Code First created a SQL Server Express database. Code First's database connection handling ranges from this completely automated behavior to creating a database for you at a location designated in a connection string. There are a lot of variations to being able to drop and recreate a database when your model changes during development.

You'll find that Chapter 6 is dedicated entirely to how Code First interacts with your database.

The examples in this book will walk you through how to configure database mappings. These concepts apply equally to generating a database or mapping to an existing database. When generating a database, they affect the schema that is generated for you. When mapping to an existing database, they define the schema that Entity Framework will expect to be there at runtime.

As we explore Code First conventions and configuration in this book, we will be allowing Code First to create a database. This allows you to run the application after each step and observe how the database schema has changed. If you are mapping to an existing database, the only difference is to point Code First at that database. The easiest way to do that is described in "Controlling Database Location with a Configuration File" on page 130 (Chapter 6). You will also want to take a look at "Reverse Engineer Code First" on page 173 (Chapter 8).

What Code First Does Not Support

Code First is a relatively new addition to Entity Framework and there are a few features that it currently does not support. The EF team has indicated that they plan to add support for most of these in future releases.

Database migrations

At the time of writing this book, Code First does not yet support database migrations, or in other words, modifying a database to reflect changes to the model. But work on this feature is well under way and will likely be available shortly after publication. You can read about an early preview of the Migrations support on the team's blog (*http://blogs.msdn.com/b/adonet/archive/2011/09/21/code-first-migra tions -alpha-3-released.aspx*).

Mapping to views

Code First currently only supports mapping to tables. This unfortunately means that you can't map Code First directly to stored procedures, views, or other database objects. If you are letting Code First generate a database, there is no way to create these artifacts in the database, other than manually adding them once Code First has created the database. If you are mapping to an existing database, there are some techniques you can use to get data from non-table database artifacts.

These techniques are described in "Mapping to Nontable Database Objects" on page 153 (Chapter 7).

Schema definition defining queries

Entity Framework includes a `DefiningQuery` feature that allows you to specify a database query directly in the XML metadata. There is also a Query View feature that allows you to use the conceptual model to define a query that is used to load entities. This allows the query you specify to be database provider–independent. Code First does not support either of these features yet.

Multiple Entity Sets per Type (MEST)

Code First does not support the Multiple Entity Sets per Type (MEST) feature. MEST allows you to use the same class in two different sets that map to two different tables. This is a more obscure Entity Framework feature that is rarely used. The EF team has said that, in an effort to keep the Code First API simpler, they do not plan to add support for MEST.

Conditional column mapping

When working with inheritance hierarchies, Code First also requires that a property is always mapped to a column with the same name. This is referred to as *conditional column mapping*. For example, you may have a `Person` base class with a `NationalIdentifier` property. `American` and `Australian` classes that derive from the `Person` base class are mapped to separate `Australians` and `Americans` tables in the database. When using the designer, you could map the `NationalIdentifier` property to an `SSN` column in the `Americans` table and `PassportNumber` in the `Australians` table. Code First does not support this scenario. The column that `NationalIdentifier` maps to must have the same name in every table.

Choosing Code First

Now that you know what Code First is, you may be wondering whether it's the right modeling workflow for your application development. The good news is that the decision is almost entirely dependent on what development style you, or your team, prefer.

If writing your own POCO classes and then using code to define how they map to a database appeals to you, then Code First is what you are after. As mentioned earlier, Code First can generate a database for you or be used to map to an existing database.

If you prefer to use a designer to define the shape of your classes and how they map to the database, you probably don't want to use Code First. If you are mapping to an existing database, you will want to use Database First to reverse engineer a model from the database. This entails using Visual Studio's Entity Data Model Wizard to generate an EDMX based on that database. You can then view and edit the generated model using the designer. If you don't have a database but want to use a designer, you should consider using Model First to define your model with the designer. You can then create the database based on the model you define. These approaches work well, provided you are happy for EF to generate your classes for you based on the model you create in the designer.

Finally, if you have existing classes that you want to use with EF, you probably want to go with Code First even if your first preference would be for designer-based modeling. If you choose to use the designer, you will need to make any model changes in the designer and in your classes. This is inefficient and error-prone, so you will probably be happier in the long run if you use Code First. In Code First, your classes are your model, so model changes only need to be made in one place and there is no opportunity for things to get out of sync.

> A designer tool that the Entity Framework team is working on will provide an additional option—reverse engineering a database into Code First classes and fluent configurations. This tool was created for developers who have an existing database but prefer using Code First to using a designer. You'll learn more about this tool in Chapter 8.

The decision process for which EF workflow to use can be summarized in the decision tree shown in Figure 1-5.

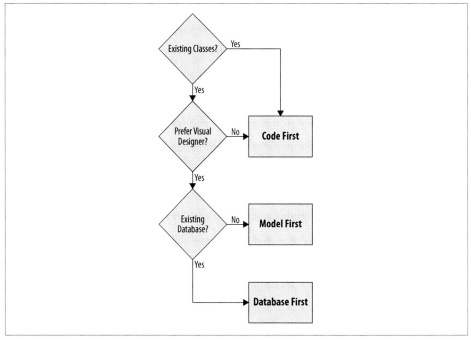

Figure 1-5. Workflow decision tree

Learning from This Book

This book will focus on building and configuring a model with Code First. It is an extension to *Programming Entity Framework* (second edition) and you'll find many references back to that book, rather than duplicating here the nearly 900 pages of detailed information about how Entity Framework functions; how to query and update; using it in a variety of application types and automated tests; and how to handle exceptions, security, database connections and transactions. Creating a model with Code First is just one more feature of the Entity Framework.

In fact, as you move forward to Chapter 2, you'll find that the domain model changes from the veterinarian sample used in Chapter 1 to the business model of *Programming Entity Framework*, software applications built for a company called Break Away Geek Adventures.

Look for a second short book titled *Programming Entity Framework: DbContext*, which will focus on `DbContext`, `DbSet`, Validation API, and using the features that are also part of the Entity Framework NuGet package.

CHAPTER 2

Your First Look at Code First

If you've worked with either the first or second edition of *Programming Entity Framework*, you may recall the business that was the focus of the book sample—Break Away Geek Adventures, also known as BAGA. BAGA coordinates much-needed adventure travel for geeks like us. But it's been a few years, and the business is growing again, so it's time for some new apps. And since BAGA caters to software geeks, they can't resist an excuse to try out a new technology such as EF's Code First.

In this chapter, we'll start with a small example to witness some of Code First's default behavior and then add to this example bit by bit to see how each thing we do impacts this behavior.

We'll begin with a small slice of BAGA's business domain: the Destinations of our trips and the Lodgings where our geek clients stay on these trips.

The beauty of Code First is that the code we use to define our domain classes is the same code that is used to describe the data model on which Entity Framework relies. And that's just where we will start—with the code, shown in Example 2-1, which describes the Destination and Lodging classes. For these early examples, we'll keep the classes very simple; they'll contain some auto-implemented properties and no further logic.

Example 2-1. The domain model

```
public class Destination
{
  public int DestinationId { get; set; }
  public string Name { get; set; }
  public string Country { get; set; }
  public string Description { get; set; }
  public byte[] Photo { get; set; }

  public List<Lodging> Lodgings { get; set; }
}

public class Lodging
{
```

```
  public int LodgingId { get; set; }
  public string Name { get; set; }
  public string Owner { get; set; }
  public bool IsResort { get; set; }

  public Destination Destination { get; set; }
}
```

The Destination class describes a particular locale where a BAGA trip might go. At any given destination, from Aspen to Zimbabwe, BAGA has made arrangements with various lodgings, from bed and breakfasts to five-star hotels, where clients will stay. So a destination object can have one or more lodgings—List<Lodging>—associated with it.

Introducing EF to the Domain Classes

On their own, these classes have nothing to do with Entity Framework or with Code First. They simply describe part of a domain.

In order for Entity Framework be aware of these classes, we'll use an Entity Framework context to serve up, manage, and persist the data to a database. EF has two contexts to choose from, the ObjectContext, which has been part of Entity Framework since its first release, and the lighter-weight DbContext, which was introduced along with Code First in Entity Framework 4.1. While it's possible to use ObjectContext, it is more common (and recommended) to use the new DbContext with Code First, and that's what we'll be using here. Later in this book (Chapter 7), you'll learn about using ObjectContext with Code First.

Our class, BreakAwayContext, will inherit from DbContext in order to gain all of DbContext's capabilities. Additionally, it will expose properties that return queryable sets, DbSets, of Destination classes and Lodging classes.

Example 2-2. The BreakAwayContext class

```
public class BreakAwayContext : DbContext
{
  public DbSet<Destination> Destinations { get; set; }
  public DbSet<Lodging> Lodgings { get; set; }
}
```

This small class represents a complete data layer that you can use in applications. Thanks to the DbContext, you'll be able to query, change, track, and save destination and lodging data. Let's create a little console app to do some work with this data layer so you can see that this is no exaggeration.

Putting the Pieces Together in an Example

To see all of this in action, the following section will walk you through creating a small solution in Visual Studio, where you'll place these classes and then create a simplistic

---

console application to exercise your new data layer. To be sure you're starting on the right architectural path, this walkthrough will organize the layers of the application into separate projects.

1. Create a new solution in Visual Studio.
2. Add a Class Library project to the solution named Model.
3. In this project, add a new class named `Destination`.
4. Modify the `Destination` class to match the Example 2-3.

Example 2-3. The Destination class

```
using System.Collections.Generic;

namespace Model
{
    public class Destination
    {
        public int DestinationId { get; set; }
        public string Name { get; set; }
        public string Country { get; set; }
        public string Description { get; set; }

        public byte[] Photo { get; set; }

        public List<Lodging> Lodgings { get; set; }
    }
}
```

5. Add another class, named `Lodging`, to this project with the code shown in Example 2-4.

Example 2-4. The Lodging class

```
namespace Model
{
    public class Lodging
    {
        public int LodgingId { get; set; }

        public string Name { get; set; }
        public string Owner { get; set; }
        public bool IsResort { get; set; }

        public Destination Destination { get; set; }
    }
}
```

That's the extent of the Model project. Now, on to the data layer. While the domain classes have no awareness of the Entity Framework, the data layer is completely dependent on it.

1. Add another Class Library project, named DataAccess, to the solution.
2. Right-click the new project in Solution Explorer and choose Add Library Package Reference.
3. In the Add Library Package Reference dialog, select the Online tab and search for Entity Framework.
4. Click the Install button for the Entity Framework package. This will add the Code First runtime (*EntityFramework.dll*) to your project.
5. Right-click the new project in Solution Explorer and choose Add Reference.
6. Select the Projects tab and choose the Model project. This gives the context access to the domain classes that you just created in the Model project.
7. Add a new class file, BreakAwayContext, to this project.
8. Implement this new class as shown in Example 2-5.

Example 2-5. The BreakAwayContext class

```
using System.Data.Entity;
using Model;

namespace DataAccess
{
  public class BreakAwayContext : DbContext
  {
  public DbSet<Destination> Destinations { get; set; }
  public DbSet<Lodging> Lodgings { get; set; }
  }
}
```

Notice the using statements at the top of this class file. One is for the System.Data.Entity namespace. This is what gives you access to the DbContext and DbSet classes that are key to the BreakAwayContext class. This can be confusing because the classes in the System.Data.Entity namespace are defined in *EntityFramework.dll*, rather than *System.Data.Entity.dll*. *System.Data.Entity.dll* contains the core Entity Framework components and is included as part of the .NET Framework.

Now your data access layer for this simple demo is complete. It's time to exercise your data access with a small console application.

But wait! We haven't told the data layer where the database is. There's no connection string, no configuration file, nothing related to a database. We'll take advantage of one of Code First's capabilities—database initialization. Code First has a series of steps it follows to find a database to work with and initialize it. We'll let it use its default behavior for now, and later, in Chapter 6, you'll learn much more about database initialization features. But lest you get concerned, it is indeed possible to work with an existing database. We just won't go that route for now.

1. Add a new Console Application project to the solution, named BreakAwayConsole.
2. Right-click the new project in Solution Explorer and select Set as StartUp Project.
3. Right-click the new project in Solution Explorer again, choose Add Library Package Reference, and add a reference to the EntityFramework package.
4. Right-click the new project in Solution Explorer for the last time (we promise), choose Add Reference, and add a reference to the Model and DataAccess projects.
5. In the new project, open the Program class (Module in Visual Basic).
6. Add two using statements below the existing using statements at the top of the file:

       using Model;
       using DataAccess;

7. Add a method to the class called InsertDestination (Example 2-6).

   Example 2-6. The InsertDestination method

```
private static void InsertDestination()
{
  var destination = new Destination
      {
        Country = "Indonesia",
        Description = "EcoTourism at its best in exquisite Bali",
        Name = "Bali"
      };
  using (var context = new BreakAwayContext())
  {
    context.Destinations.Add(destination);
    context.SaveChanges();
  }
}
```

8. In the Main method of the class, call this new method (Example 2-7).

Example 2-7. Calling the InsertDestination method

```
static void Main()
{
  InsertDestination();
}
```

You're done!

With this small amount of code you've written for the two domain classes, the two-line data access class, and this little application, you are ready to roll. Run the application.

This console application doesn't bother displaying any information to you. What's interesting is what's happened in the database—the database that did not exist a moment ago.

Code First used the information it discovered in the `Destination` and `Lodging` classes to determine the model and infer the schema of the database that these classes are persisted in. Since we provided no connection string information, it uses its default convention, which is to look in the local SQL Server Express instance (*localhost \SQLEXPRESS*) for a database matching the fully qualified name of the context class —`DataAccess.BreakAwayContext`. Not finding one, Code First creates the database and then uses the model it discovered by convention to build the tables and columns of the database.

Therefore, we'll need to look in SQL Server Express for the database that Code First created (Figure 2-1).

And there it is, `DataAccess.BreakAwayContext` with a `Destinations` table and a `Lodg ings` table. That `EdmMetadata` table is used by Code First's database initialization, and you'll learn more about that later.

Convention for Table, Schema, and Column Names

Code First's convention for table naming is to use Entity Framework's Pluralization Service (introduced in Entity Framework 4) to determine the plural of the class name based on rules for the English language. By default, each table is created using the `dbo` schema.

Code First creates the columns using the same names as the class properties they map to.

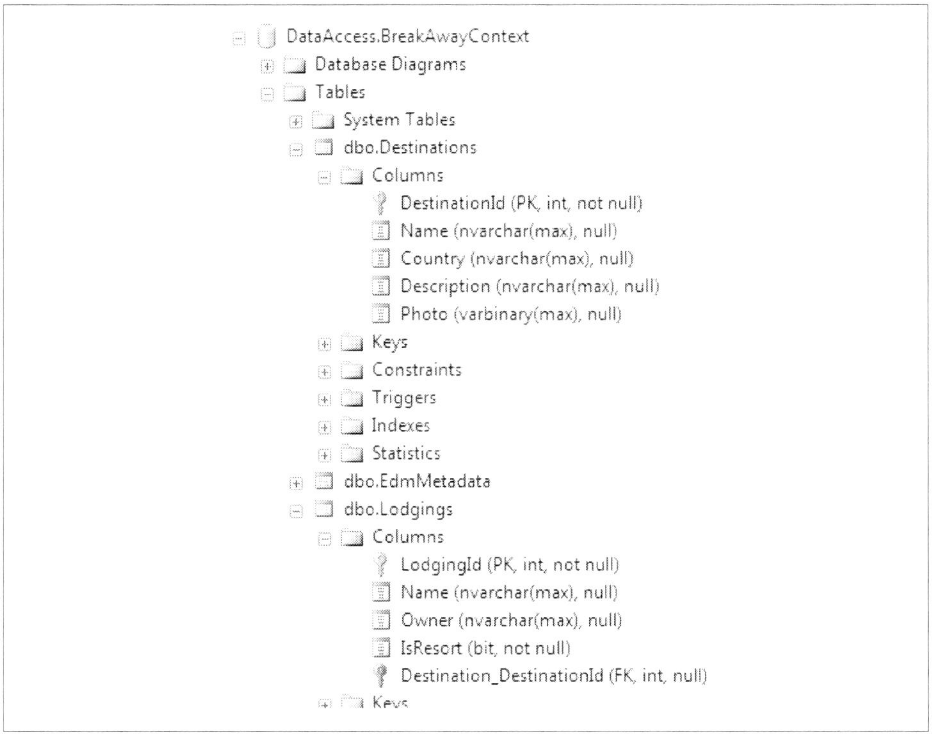

Figure 2-1. Database created by Code First

Convention for Keys

Taking a closer look at the database tables, you can learn quite a bit already about Code First conventions. For example, Code First knew that `DestinationId` in the `Destination` class and `LodgingId` in the `Lodging` class were meant to be keys and that those keys map to Primary Key fields in the database. Notice that both of these database fields are non-nullable Primary Keys (`PK, not null`). Code First convention looks for fields that are named `Id` or `[class name]Id` and determines that these are meant to be keys for the classes. `DestinationId` and `LodgingId` match this convention. Because these properties are integer types, Code First has also configured them to be identity columns in the database. This means that the database will generate values for these columns during insert.

Convention for String Properties

The convention for strings is that they map to nullable columns with no limit on length. The database provider is responsible for determining exactly which data type is used for the column. For SQL Server, the default data type for columns used to store string properties is nvarchar(max). That's why you can see in Figure 2-1 that all of the string properties from the two classes have become nvarchar(max) columns—Destina tion.Name, Country, Description, etc.—and also allow null values to be stored.

Convention for Byte Array

The Destination class has a Photo property, which is defined as a byte array (byte[]). As with string properties, Code First convention maps byte arrays to nullable columns with no limit on length. For SQL Server, this results in the varbinary(max) data type being used for the Photo column.

Convention for Booleans

The IsResort property in Lodging is a bool. Because bool is a value type, and cannot be assigned a null value, Code First presumes that the column should also not allow nulls. The SQL Server provider determines that bool properties map to the bit database type.

Convention for One-to-Many Relationships

A destination can have many lodgings and the Destination class has a List<Lodging> property to allow you to access those lodgings from a particular destination. Addition- ally, the Lodging class has a Destination property, so that you can see what Destina tion is associated with a particular Lodging. Code First recognizes this one-to-many relationship between Destination and Lodging and, by convention, determines that the Lodgings table will need a foreign key in order to persist its knowledge of which Desti nation a Lodging belongs to.

Notice that although there is no foreign key property in the Lodging class pointing back to the Destination (e.g., DestinationId), Code First created a foreign key in the database using the pattern *[Name of navigation property]_[Primary Key of related class]* (i.e., Destination_DestinationId). And thanks to some additional metadata that Code First built, Entity Framework will know to use that Foreign Key when querying from or saving to the database.

The navigation properties in the Destination and Lodging classes provide Code First with not one, but two clues about this relationship. Had we only provided one of these, the relationship would still have been obvious to Code First, which still would have created the foreign key in the database.

There are also conventions for scenarios where you've provided a foreign key, for many- to-many relationships, and more. You'll learn about these as you progress further through the book.

Overriding Convention with Configurations

As you learned in Chapter 1, Code First allows you to override its conventions by supplying additional configuration. You can choose between attribute-based Data Annotations or the strongly typed Fluent API for providing this configuration.

Any configuration you supply will be included as part of the model that Entity Framework uses to reason about your data at runtime. This not only affects the database schema but is also used by the built-in validation functionality of DbContext. For example, if you tell Code First that a property is required, the Validation API will let you know if that property has not been populated. You'll see this in action as we move forward.

Configuring with Data Annotations

Data Annotations are the simplest form of configuration and are applied directly to your classes and class properties. These attributes are available in the System.Compo nentModel.DataAnnotations namespace, which is currently distributed across the *System.ComponentModel.DataAnnotations.dll* and the *EntityFramework.dll*. In future versions of the .NET Framework, the annotations in *EntityFramework.dll* will move into *System.ComponentModel.DataAnnotations.dll*. You will need references to one or both of these assemblies (depending on which annotations you use) in the project that contains your domain classes. Be aware that the Data Annotations allow the most commonly used configuration to be performed but not all of the possible Code First configurations can be achieved with Data Annotations. Some can only be applied using the alternate style of configuring your classes—the Fluent API.

Because Code First did not automatically discover some of my intent with the Destina tion and Lodging classes, let's use some Data Annotations to provide additional configuration details.

Applying Attributes in C# and Visual Basic

In case you are new to using attributes, in C#, attributes are applied using square brackets. For example, the data annotation for identifying a Key property in C# is [Key], while in Visual Basic, angle brackets are used (<Key>). When an attribute uses a named parameter, in C# it is expressed with an equals sign ([Table(Schema="baga")]), whereas Visual Basic uses a colon in front of the equals sign (<Table(Schema:="baga")>). For more information on using attributes in .NET code, see the MSDN topic "Applying Attributes," at *http://msdn.microsoft.com/en-us/library/ bfz783fz.aspx*.

Let's start with the Destination class. There are three things I'd like to change about this class:

- Ensure that the Name is provided
- Limit the amount of text in the Description field to 500 characters.
- Store the Photo into a SQL Server image type, not a varbinary(max).

Some of the annotations I'll need for these configurations are in the *System.ComponentModel.DataAnnotations.dll* assembly that is part of .NET 4, but one will need a reference to the *EntityFramework.dll* assembly.

1. In the Model project, add a reference to the System.ComponentModel.DataAnnotations assembly.

2. Add a library package reference to this project for the EntityFramework assembly.

Remember, you'll have to use the Add Library Project Reference wizard for each project to which you want to add one of the NuGet packages, even if that package is already added to another project in your solution. Follow the same steps you did when adding *EntityFramework.dll* to the –DataAccess project.

3. At the top of the Destination class, add a using for System.ComponentModel.DataAnnotations.

4. Modify the class adding annotations to Name, Description, and Photo, as shown in Example 2-8.

Example 2-8. Modified Destination class

```
using System.Collections.Generic;
using System.ComponentModel.DataAnnotations;

namespace Model
{
  public class Destination
  {
    public int DestinationId { get; set; }
    [Required]
    public string Name { get; set; }
    public string Country { get; set; }
    [MaxLength(500)]
    public string Description { get; set; }

    [Column(TypeName="image")]
    public byte[] Photo { get; set; }

    public List<Lodging> Lodgings { get; set; }
  }
}
```

The Required annotation needs no additional information, whereas the MaxLength and Column have parameter information that you need to provide. The parameter provided to the Column annotation is specific to the database that you are mapping to. We want to store Photo in a SQL Server image field. As long as it's possible to coerce the type used for the property to the database data type you specify (e.g., coerce a byte[] to an image), you can configure the data type. All three annotations will impact the database schema and two of them, Required and MaxLength, will also be used by Entity Framework for validation. Before observing these effects, let's make some changes to the Lodging class as well.

Annotations are composable, meaning that you can apply multiple annotations to a class or property. We'll do that for the Lodging.Name property.

Add the following three annotations to the Name property in the Lodging class:

```
[Required]
[MaxLength(200)]
[MinLength(10)]
```

MinLength is an interesting annotation. While MaxLength has a database counterpart, MinLength does not. MinLength will be used for Entity Framework validation, but it won't impact the database.

 MinLength is the only configuration that can be achieved using Data Annotations but has no counterpart in the Fluent API configurations.

Understanding How Model Changes Impact Database Initialization

If you were to run the console application again, you'd get a big fat InvalidOperationException. There's nothing wrong with the model changes that we've made here. The problem is with the default behavior of Code First database initialization. So we're going to have to stop the presses, switch gears, and fix this problem before moving on with exploring configuration.

Here's the exact exception message:

> The model backing the 'BreakAwayContext' context has changed since the database was created. Either manually delete/update the database, or call Database.SetInitializer with an IDatabaseInitializer instance. For example, the DropCreateDatabaseIfModelChanges strategy will automatically delete and recreate the database, and optionally seed it with new data.

By default, Code First will create the database only if it doesn't already exist, but your database does exist.

Remember that EdmMetadata table in the database? If not, take a peek at Figure 2-1 again. That table contains a snapshot of the database section of the model that Code First built. When Code First uses a model for the first time in an application process, by default, it will go through its model building process. Then it will compare the in-memory model with the last version—which it can see by reading the EdmMetadata table. In this case, Code First recognized that the metadata of the new model does not match the metadata of the previous model and therefore cannot guarantee that your model will map to the database.

You have a number of options. One is to simply delete the database (and all of its data along with it) and let Code First use its rule (no database=create a new one, please) to recreate the database using the updated model. This can get to be a pain when you are in development and can also create file lock issues if you try to run your application too quickly after deleting the database. Another, which we will use for now, is to delete and recreate the database whenever a model change is detected by Code First. Code First has a set of initialization strategies to apply these rules for you. The default is encapsulated in a class called CreateDatabaseIfNotExists. The one we'll use is in a class called DropCreateDatabaseIfModelChanges. You can tell your executing application (in this case, the console app) which strategy to use. Here's how we'll do it.

Modify the Main method adding in the code shown in Example 2-9 above InsertDestination. You'll need to add a using statement for System.Data.Entity as well.

Example 2-9. Adding Database Initialization to the Main method

```
static void Main(string[] args)
{
  Database.SetInitializer(
    new DropCreateDatabaseIfModelChanges<BreakAwayContext>());
  InsertDestination();
}
```

In this code we're telling Code First to use an initializer and specifying which strategy to use (DropCreateDatabaseIfModelChanges) and on which context (BreakAwayContext). Now when you rerun the application, Code First will recognize the difference in the new model and, with permission from the initializer, will delete and recreate the database when the time comes.

If you've opened up the database tables to read data somewhere else (for example, in Visual Studio's Server Explorer), Code First will not be able to delete the database. In this case, there will be a delay while it attempts the delete, and then eventually EF will get the message from the database and an exception will be thrown. I seem to do this too frequently when I'm demonstrating at user groups and conferences.

A common scenario I encounter is that I have opened up SQL Server Management Studio (SSMS) and performed some queries on the database. Closing the query windows releases the database. You shouldn't have to close SSMS completely to release its clutches on the database.

The new database is shown in Figure 2-2.

```
□ 目 DataAccess.BreakAwayContext
  ⊞ □ Database Diagrams
  □ □ Tables
    ⊞ □ System Tables
    □ □ dbo.Destinations
      □ □ Columns
          ♀ DestinationId (PK, int, not null)
          ▣ Name (nvarchar(max), not null)
          ▣ Country (nvarchar(max), null)
          ▣ Description (nvarchar(500), null)
          ▣ Photo (image, null)
      ⊞ □ Keys
      ⊞ □ Constraints
      ⊞ □ Triggers
      ⊞ □ Indexes
      ⊞ □ Statistics
    ⊞ □ dbo.EdmMetadata
    □ □ dbo.Lodgings
      □ □ Columns
          ♀ LodgingId (PK, int, not null)
          ▣ Name (nvarchar(200), not null)
          ▣ Owner (nvarchar(max), null)
          ▣ IsResort (bit, not null)
          ♀ Destination_DestinationId (FK, int, null)
```

Figure 2-2. Destinations and Lodgings tables after model changes

The three changes we made to the Destination class are now visible in the Destinations table. Name, which we set to Required, is now non-nullable in the database. Description is now an nvarchar(500) rather than max and Photo is an image data type.

The Lodgings table has also been affected. Name is now limited to 200 characters and is non-nullable. The third annotation applied to Name, MinLength, has no equivalent in the database schema, so it is ignored here. Remember, though, Entity Framework will pay attention to that attribute when it is validating Lodging objects.

Data Annotations and Validation-Aware UIs

Data Annotations were introduced in .NET 4 for use in validation-aware UIs such as ASP.NET MVC and ASP.NET Dynamic Data. Many of the annotations you'll use for your Code First classes come from this same set of annotations that live in the System.ComponentModel.DataAnnotations assembly. Therefore, those UIs will respond to invalid data where the validation is based on one of the annotations from this assembly.

For example, the Required annotation is in the .NET 4 assembly, not the *EntityFramework.dll* assembly. Therefore, if you are using your Code First classes in an MVC application and the user has neglected to fill out a field that is bound to a Required property, the MVC UI validation will respond, as you can see in Figure 2-3.

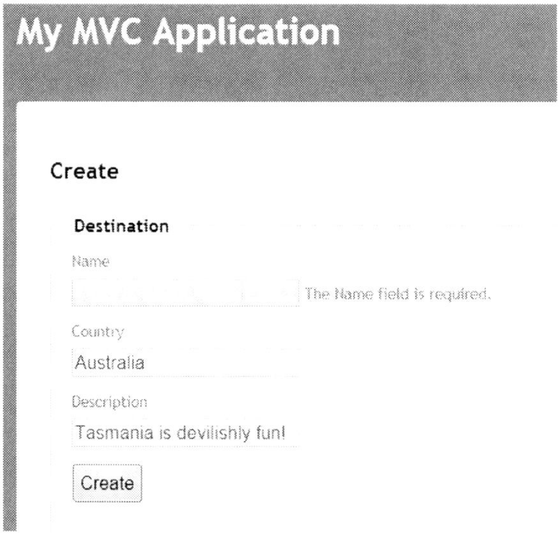

My MVC Application

Create

Destination

Name

    The Name field is required.

Country

Australia

Description

Tasmania is devilishly fun!

Create

Figure 2-3. The Required Data Annotation being picked up by MVC validation

DbContext also provides a Validation API, so there is also server-side validation happening, whether you configure with Data Annotations or the Fluent API. But when you are using Data Annotations that are also tracked by MVC, MVC will pick them up as well. The Validation API is not covered in this book, which focuses on modeling with Code First, but it will be part of the partner book, *Entity Framework: DbContext*.

Configuring Code First with the Fluent API

Configuring with Data Annotations is fairly simple and it may be just what you're looking for. But Data Annotations only allow you to access a subset of the possible configurations (though much more than you've seen so far). The Fluent API, however, gives you access to even more, so you may prefer it for this reason.

What Is a Fluent API?

The concept of a fluent API isn't specific to Code First or the Entity Framework. The fundamental idea behind a fluent API involves using chained method calls to produce code that is easy for the developer to read. The return type of each call then defines the valid methods for the next call. For example, in the Code First Fluent API, you can use the `Entity` method to select an entity to configure. IntelliSense will then show you all the methods that can be used to configure an `Entity`. If you then use the `Property` method to select a property to configure, you will see all the methods available for configuring that particular property.

There's another reason why some developers will prefer the Fluent API over the annotations. While applying annotations to your pretty domain classes, they can definitely get more and more bogged down with the attributes. It's one thing to be applying validation logic (`Required`, `MaxLength`, etc.), but as you learn more about configuration options, you'll see that there are also many that are specifically about how the class maps to the database. If you prefer cleaner classes, you may not want the class to include information about what table name it should map to in the database. One of the benefits that many developers see in Code First is that it allows you to use Entity Framework with classes that are persistence-ignorant. A class that includes database table names or column data types is not at all ignorant of how it's being persisted. The Fluent API allows you to associate the configurations with the context rather than the classes themselves. The classes remain clean. Let's see how this works.

Following the Data Annotations and Fluent API Walkthroughs

Throughout the rest of this book, you will see many examples of how to configure mappings using Data Annotations and how to configure them using the Fluent API. Some mappings can only be achieved with the Fluent API.

If you are following along with the examples in Visual Studio, we highly recommend that you do so in two separate solutions. Otherwise, when you code a Data Annotation and then want to see the same effect in Fluent configurations, you'll have to comment out the Data Annotation. Then, when you move forward to another annotation, you'll have to comment out the Fluent configurations. It won't take long for the jumble of commented and uncommented code to cross wires and throw error messages that occur because of overlapping or completely missing configurations.

This will mean some required copy/pasting when we have you add a new class or add a new method to the solution. But it also means Data Annotations will only be applied in one solution and Fluent configurations will be restricted to the other.

If you do follow this advice, there is one additional suggestion we have for you: Be sure to use different namespace names for the BreakAwayContext class in the two solutions. That way if one solution uses the namespace DataLayerForAnnotations, its database will be DataLayerForAnnotations.BreakAwayContext. If the other uses DataLayerForFluent, its database name will be DataLayerForFluent.BreakAwayContext. You will be happier to have two separate databases and a clear understanding of which solution is impacting which database.

When it's time to build the model, the DbContext first looks at the classes and learns what it can from them. At this point, the context is ready to reason out the model, but there is an opportunity for the developer to interrupt the context and perform additional configuration. This is thanks to the DbContext.OnModelCreating method, which is called by the context just before the model is built. The method is virtual, so you can override it and insert your own logic. This is where the Fluent API configurations go.

The signature of this method is as follows:

```
protected override void OnModelCreating(DbModelBuilder modelBuilder)
```

The DbModelBuilder that is provided to the OnModelCreating method is the class that allows you to add configurations. The DbModelBuilder leverages generics and lambdas so you'll get plenty of strong typing to help you along while coding the configurations.

The basic pattern is to tell the DbModelBuilder which entity (class) you want to configure:

```
modelBuilder.Entity<Destination>()
```

You can configure the class itself (e.g., what database table it maps to):

```
modelBuilder.Entity<Destination>().ToTable("a_table_name")
```

You can also configure properties of the class. If you want to configure a property, you have to drill in further:

```
modelBuilder.Entity<Destination>()
        .Property(d => d.Description).HasMaxLength(500)
```

The code in Example 2-10 replicates all of the configuration that we previously performed using the data annotations. OnModelCreating is a method of DbContext, so be sure to put it in your BreakAwayContext class.

Example 2-10. Configuring with the Fluent API

```
protected override void OnModelCreating(DbModelBuilder modelBuilder)
{
  modelBuilder.Entity<Destination>()
    .Property(d => d.Name).IsRequired();
  modelBuilder.Entity<Destination>()
```

```
    .Property(d => d.Description).HasMaxLength(500);
  modelBuilder.Entity<Destination>()
    .Property(d => d.Photo).HasColumnType("image");

  modelBuilder.Entity<Lodging>()
    .Property(l => l.Name).IsRequired().HasMaxLength(200);
}
```

Some of the configurations are composable. Notice that the configuration for Lodg
ing.Name combines IsRequired with HasMaxLength.

 If you are wondering where HasMinLength is, there is no Fluent configuration for minimum length, as it is not a facet of a database column.

While it's possible to use a combination of Data Annotations and the Fluent API, it
makes most sense to use one or the other to keep your code consistent. For this example,
since the configuration is now coded fluently, we've removed all of the Data Annotations. In fact the Model project no longer needs the references to the System.Component
Model.DataAnnotations or EntityFramework assemblies.

When running the example again, Code First will compare the model to the EdmMeta
data table in the database and see that although we changed how we configured the
model, the end result is the same. Therefore it will not need to drop and create the
database. The same destination will get added to the database again, so you'll end up
with matching records. You can see the duplicate data in Figure 2-4.

DestinationId	Name	Country	Description	Photo
1	Bali	Indonesia	Eco Tourism at it's best in the exquisite Bali	NULL
2	Bali	Indonesia	Eco Tourism at it's best in the exquisite Bali	NULL

Figure 2-4. Duplicate data from InsertDestination being rerun without recreating the database

Organizing Fluent Configurations

If you have a lot of configuration to perform, the OnModelCreating method might quickly
become overwhelmed with code. You can group configuration by entity type within
individual EntityTypeConfiguration classes, and then tell the DbModelBuilder about
them in the OnModelCreating method. DbModelBuilder has a Configurations property to
which you can add these EntityTypeConfigurations.

Example 2-11 shows all of the configurations for the Destination class grouped into
the DestinationConfiguration class and the same for the Lodging configurations.

Example 2-11. Organizing configs into separate EntityTypeConfiguration classes

```
using System.Data.Entity.ModelConfiguration;
using Model;

public class DestinationConfiguration :
  EntityTypeConfiguration<Destination>
{
  public DestinationConfiguration()
  {
    Property(d => d.Name).IsRequired();
    Property(d => d.Description).HasMaxLength(500);
    Property(d => d.Photo).HasColumnType("image");
  }
}
public class LodgingConfiguration :
 EntityTypeConfiguration<Lodging>
{
  public LodgingConfiguration()
  {
    Property(l => l.Name).IsRequired().HasMaxLength(200);
  }
}
```

When these were inside the OnModelCreating method, they began with the DbModel Builder, followed by the Entity method to identify which entity was being configured. But in an EntityConfiguration class, that is already known, based on the fact that the class is inheriting from EntityTypeConfiguration and the entity type is specified. Therefore, rather than, for example, modelBuilder.Entity<Destination>().Property, you begin with Property. Calling modelBuilder.Entity<Destination>() will actually create an EntityTypeConfiguration<Destination> and return it to you, so whichever approach you chose, you are accessing the same API.

And now in Example 2-12, you can see the revised OnModelCreating method that consumes these classes.

Example 2-12. Adding the configuration classes in OnModelCreating

```
protected override void OnModelCreating(DbModelBuilder modelBuilder)
{
  modelBuilder.Configurations.Add(new DestinationConfiguration());
  modelBuilder.Configurations.Add(new LodgingConfiguration());
}
```

As we move forward with fluent configuration examples in this book, we'll sometimes show the configuration as it would look inside an `Enti tyTypeConfiguration` class and other times show the configuration as a `modelBuilder` configuration. This is just for the sake of letting you continue to see both syntaxes. However, in your production applications, it is more reasonable not to mix up the placement of your configuration. You will most likely want to have a consistent pattern, whether that means putting all of the configuration inside the `OnModelCreating` method or always organizing them into `EntityTypeConfiguration` classes. You'll see that there are a few configuration operations that are not type-specific and must go directly in the `OnModelCreating` method.

Summary

In this chapter you have seen the basics of working with Code First. You've learned that Code First's conventional behavior is quite intelligent, with the ability to guess what your intention is based on what it discovers in your classes. When the convention is not able to infer correctly, you can explicitly control how Code First builds a model and database schema by applying configuration. You learned about configuring directly in the class by applying attributes called Data Annotations. For those who prefer to leave their domain classes alone, you learned how to use the alternative Fluent API to perform configuration in the `DbContext` class.

Code First can automatically build a database for you. You've seen how to exert some control over its response to changes you make in the model with respect to recreating the database to match the new model.

Now that you've got the flavor of how Code First works, we'll dig further into all of these topics as we move through the rest of the chapters, expanding the model and learning the ins and outs of modeling with Code First.

CHAPTER 3

Using Conventions and Configurations for Property Attributes

In Chapter 2, you got your first look at some of Code First's conventions and how to override Code First's default behavior with configuration. You not only saw how to configure with Data Annotations, but we also applied the same configuration using the Fluent API so you could see a direct comparison.

In this and the next few chapters, we'll walk you through a variety of areas where you can configure your model. For each topic you'll see what Code First does by convention and then you'll learn how to override the convention with Data Annotations and the Fluent API. As you've learned, there are a number of configurations you can apply using the Fluent API that are not available with Data Annotations. We'll be sure to point out those cases when it's time to dig into them.

We'll kick things off in this chapter by focusing on Code First conventions and configuration that affect attributes of the properties and their related database columns. You'll learn about working with attributes such as the length of a string or byte array and precision of numeric values. You'll work with key properties and properties that are involved with optimistic concurrency. Finally, you'll learn about how Code First detects when a property is in fact a *complex type* (aka *value type*), as well as how to help when it's unable to infer these complex types from your domain classes.

Working with Property Attributes in Code First

In Chapter 2, you saw some of Code First's conventions and configuration options that apply to string properties. We'll provide a quick review here before moving on to new attributes.

Length

Convention	max (type specified by database)
Data Annotation	MinLength(*nn*)
	MaxLength(*nn*)
	StringLength(*nn*)
Fluent	Entity<T>.Property(t=>t.PropertyName).HasMaxLength(nn)

Length is used to describe the length of arrays. Currently that encompasses `string` and `Byte` array.

Code First convention specifies that the length of string or byte array should be `max`. The database provider then determines what type should be used. In SQL Server, `string` becomes `nvarchar(max)` and byte array becomes `varbinary(max)`.

You can override the default length, which will impact the length used in the database. The maximum length of a property is also validated by Entity Framework at runtime before pushing changes to the database. With Data Annotations, you can also configure a `MinLength` attribute for an array. `MinLength` will get validated by Entity Framework's Validation API but will not impact the database.

The StringLength Alternative

`MinLength` and `MaxLength` are part of the *EntityFramework.dll*. There is also a `String Length` annotation that is part of the *System.ComponentModel.DataAnnotations.dll*:

```
[StringLength(500,MinimumLength= 10)]
public string Description { get; set; }
```

Code First will recognize this annotation if you prefer to use it. If you are working with ASP.NET MVC or Dynamic Data, they will recognize `StringLength`, but they will not know about `MinLength` and `MaxLength` from the *EntityFramework.dll*.

 When running against SQL Compact Edition, there is an additional convention that replaces the default maximum array length with `4000` rather than `Max`.

Data Type

Convention	The default column data type is determined by the database provider you are using. For SQL Server some example default data types are:
	String : nvarchar(max)

	Integer : int
	Byte Array : varbinary(max)
	Boolean : bit
Data Annotation	Column(TypeName="*xxx*")
Fluent	Entity<T>.Property(t=>t.*PropertyName*).HasColumnType ("*xxx*")

In Chapter 2, you saw a number of examples of how Code First maps .NET types to data types. The `Destination` and `Lodging` classes contain `Integer`s, `String`s, a `Byte` array, and a `Boolean`. Code First lets the database provider select the appropriate data type to use for each column. The application is using the SQL Server database provider, which mapped those to `nvarchar(max)`, `int`, `varbinary(max)`, and `bit`, respectively.

It's possible to map to a different database type using configurations as long as you choose a database type that can be cast automatically. For example, if you try to set the data type of a `String` to a database `int`, at runtime the `DbModelBuilder` will throw an error saying `Member Mapping specified is not valid`, followed by details of the .NET type and the database type you were attempting to coerce it to.

In Chapter 2, we changed the database type of the `Photo` property to be an `image` type rather than a `varbinary(max)`.

Nullability and the Required Configuration

Convention	Key Properties : not null in database
	Reference Types (String, arrays): null in the database
	Value Types (all numeric types, DateTime, bool, char) : not null in database
	Nullable<T> Value Types : null in database
Data Annotation	Required
Fluent	Entity<T>.Property(t=>t.*PropertyName*).IsRequired

Convention will ensure that .NET types that are non-nullable map to non-nullable fields in the database. Additionally, any properties that are part of the key will map to non-nullable database fields.

If you use .NET to specify a value type (such as `int`) to be nullable using the generic `Nullable<T>`, it will map to a nullable database field.

You saw in Chapter 2 how to specify that a property is required using configuration. You used the Required Data Annotation and then the `IsRequired` Fluent configuration to force the `Lodging.Name` property to be required. Required properties are validated by the Entity Framework at runtime before saving data to the database; an exception is thrown if the property has not been populated.

Another effect is that when you mark a property as `Required`, its database field will become not null.

Mapping Keys

Convention	Properties named Id
	Properties named [TypeName] + Id
Data Annotation	Key
Fluent	Entity<T>.HasKey(t=>t.*PropertyName*)

Entity Framework requires every entity to have a key. This key is used by the context to keep track of individual objects. Keys are unique and often generated by the database. Code First convention makes these same presumptions.

Recall that when Code First created the database from the `Destination` and `Lodging` classes, the `DestinationId` and `LodgingId int` fields in the resulting tables were marked PK and not null. If you look further into the column properties for `DestinationId` and `LodgingId`, you'll see that these two fields are also Auto-Incremented Identity fields, as shown in Figure 3-1. This, too, is by convention for integers that are primary keys.

Identity Specification	Yes
(Is Identity)	Yes
Identity Increment	1
Identity Seed	1

Figure 3-1. An auto-incremented identity key in the database

Most commonly, primary keys in the database are either `int` or `GUID` types, although any primitive type can be used as a key property. A primary key in the database can be composed from multiple fields in the table, and, similarly, an entity's key can be composed of multiple properties in a particular class. At the end of this section, you'll see how to configure composite keys.

Code First Convention Response to Unconventional Key Properties

In the case of our two classes, the properties that are meant to be keys happen to meet Code First convention, so everything worked out nicely. What if they did not meet convention?

Let's add a new class to the model, `Trip`, shown in Example 3-1. The `Trip` class does not have any properties that meet the convention for an entity key, but our intent is that the `Identifier` property be used as the key.

Example 3-1. The Trip class without an obvious key property

```
public class Trip
{
  public Guid Identifier { get; set; }
  public DateTime StartDate { get; set; }
  public DateTime EndDate { get; set; }
  public decimal CostUSD { get; set; }
}
```

Along with the new class, we'll need a `DbSet<Trip>` added into `BreakAwayContext`:

```
public DbSet<Trip> Trips { get; set; }
```

When running the application again, an exception will be thrown as the `DbModel Builder` attempts to construct a model from the classes:

> One or more validation errors were detected during model generation: System.Data.Edm.EdmEntityType: :

> EntityType 'Trip' has no key defined. Define the key for this EntityType.

Because there was no key property that met the pattern expected by convention (in this case either `Id` or `TripId`), Code First could not go forward with building the model. To be clear, the type (`Guid`) has nothing to do with this problem. As stated earlier, you can use any primitive type for a key.

Configuring the Key with Data Annotations

The Data Annotation for identifying a key is simply `Key`. `Key` exists in the *System.ComponentModel.DataAnnotations.dll* because it has been added to .NET 4 for use by other APIs (for example, ASP.NET MVC uses `Key`). If your project didn't already contain a reference to this assembly, you'd need to add it. The *EntityFramework.dll* reference is not required for this particular annotation, although you might be using others from that assembly:

```
[Key]
public Guid Identifier { get; set; }
```

Don't forget that you'll need to add a `using` or `Imports` statement for the `System.ComponentModel.DataAnnotations` namespace at the top of this class.

Using HasKey to Configure a Key Property in the Fluent API

Configuring a `Key` property with the Fluent API is a bit different than the few Fluent configurations you used in Chapter 2. Rather than configuring a particular property, this configuration is added directly to the Entity. To configure a key, you use the `HasKey` method, as shown in Example 3-2.

Example 3-2. The HasKey Fluent configuration in OnModelCreating

```
modelBuilder.Entity<Trip>().HasKey(t => t.Identifier)
```

If you are encapsulating the configurations within `EntityTypeConfiguration` classes, as you learned about in Chapter 2, you begin with `HasKey` or `this.HasKey` (Example 3-3).

Example 3-3. HasKey inside of an EntityTypeConfiguration class

```
HasKey(t => t.Identifier)
```

Configuring Database-Generated Properties

Convention	Integer keys: Identity
Data Annotation	DatabaseGenerated(*DatabaseGeneratedOption*)
Fluent	Entity<T>.Property(t=>t.*PropertyName*)
	.HasDatabaseGeneratedOption(*DatabaseGeneratedOption*)

In the previous section, you learned that by default, Code First will flag `int` key properties so that Entity Framework is aware that the database will generate the values. What about the `Guid` key that we just created? `Guids` require special handling, which involves the `DatabaseGenerated` configuration.

To demonstrate, we'll add a new method, `InsertTrip` (Example 3-4) to the console application and call it from the `Main` module.

Example 3-4. The InsertTrip method

```
private static void InsertTrip()
{
  var trip = new Trip
               {
                 CostUSD = 800,
                 StartDate = new DateTime(2011, 9, 1),
                 EndDate = new DateTime(2011, 9, 14)
               };
  using (var context = new BreakAwayContext())
  {
    context.Trips.Add(trip);
    context.SaveChanges();
  }
}
```

Running the application will cause the database to be dropped and recreated with the new `Trips` table shown in Figure 3-2.

Identifier is a primary key, unique identifier, not null column.

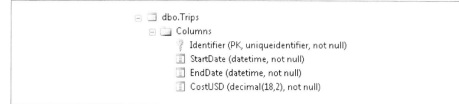

Figure 3-2. Identifier primary key in the Trips table

 Recall that earlier in the chapter, you learned that value types are required by convention. You can see the effect of this. The `StartDate`, `EndDate`, and `CostUSD` properties of the `Trip` class are all value types and therefore, by default, not null in the `Trips` table in the database.

However, an empty `Guid` value got entered into the new row. As you can see in Figure 3-3, it's filled with 0s.

	Identifier	StartDate	EndDate	CostUSD
1	00000000-0000-0000-0000-000000000000	2011-09-01 00:00:00.000	2011-09-14 00:00:00.000	800.00

Figure 3-3. Identifier without an actual Guid value

Neither the database nor Entity Framework is aware that we'd like one of them to generate a new `Guid` for new `Trips`. With no logic to generate a new `Guid` for this property, it inserted the `Guid` default value—the zeros.

If you attempt to insert another record with the same value in `Identifier`, the database will throw an error because it expects a unique value.

It is possible to configure the database to automatically generate a new `Guid`, by setting the default value to `newid()`. Whether you do this manually in the database or expect Code First to inject this logic, you must let Code First know that the database will be handling the `Guid`.

The solution is to let Code First know that the database will generate this key using another annotation: `DatabaseGenerated`. This configuration has three options—`None`, `Identity`, and `Computed`. We want the identifier to be treated as an `Identity` key by the database, forcing the database to generate the identity key values for new rows, just as it does by default with keys that are integers.

Configuring Database-Generated Options with Data Annotations

Modify the class to tell Code First that the database will generate an identity key on your behalf:

```
[Key,DatabaseGenerated(DatabaseGeneratedOption.Identity)]
public Guid Identifier { get; set; }
```

In the case where the Key field is an Integer, Code First defaults to DatabaseGeneratedOption.Identity. With a Guid, you need to explicitly configure this. These are the only types that you can configure to be Identity when Code First is generating the database. If you are mapping to an existing database, any column where the database generates a value on insert can be marked as Identity.

After running the application again, Figure 3-4 shows the newly generated Identifier.

	Identifier	StartDate	EndDate	CostUSD
1	672CCBE2-2CF7-4616-B809-175C838BCD89	2011-09-01 00:00:00.000	2011-09-14 00:00:00.000	800.00

Figure 3-4. Identifier Guid populated by the database after an EF insert

You might be interested in seeing the SQL, shown in Example 3-5, sent to the database for the INSERT where Entity Framework expects the database to generate the Guid value for the Identifier property.

Example 3-5. SQL for inserting a new Trip

```
declare @generated_keys table([Identifier] uniqueidentifier)
insert [dbo].[Trips]([StartDate], [EndDate], [CostUSD])
output inserted.[Identifier] into @generated_keys
values (@0, @1, @2)
select t.[Identifier]
from @generated_keys as g
join [dbo].[Trips] as t on g.[Identifier] = t.[Identifier]
where @@ROWCOUNT > 0',
N'@0 datetime2(7),@1 datetime2(7),@2 decimal(18,2)',
@0='2011-09-01 00:00:00',@1='2011-09-14 00:00:00',@2=800.00
```

There are two other enums for DatabaseGeneratedOption: None and Computed. Following is an example of where None is useful.

Example 3-6 shows another new class for our model, Person. The SocialSecurityNum ber property has been configured as the Key property for the class.

Example 3-6. Person class with unconventional key property

```
using System.ComponentModel.DataAnnotations;

namespace Model
{
  public class Person
  {
    [Key]
    public int SocialSecurityNumber { get; set; }
    public string FirstName { get; set; }
    public string LastName { get; set; }
```

```
  }
}
```

Remember to add a DbSet<Person> to BreakAwayContext:

```
    public DbSet<Person> People { get; set; }
```

And finally, a new method, InsertPerson (shown in Example 3-7) is added to the console app, along with a call to this from the Main method, which inserts a new person into the database.

Example 3-7. InsertPerson method

```
private static void InsertPerson()
{
  var person = new Person
  {
    FirstName = "Rowan",
    LastName = "Miller",
    SocialSecurityNumber = 12345678
  };
  using (var context = new BreakAwayContext())
  {
    context.People.Add(person);
    context.SaveChanges();
  }
}
```

After running the application again, let's take a look at the new row in the database, shown in Figure 3-5.

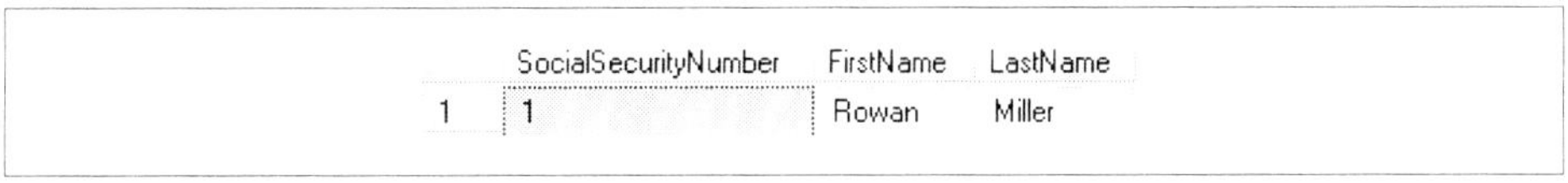

	SocialSecurityNumber	FirstName	LastName
1	1	Rowan	Miller

Figure 3-5. SocialSecurityNumber incorrectly generated

The SocialSecurityNumber is 1, not 12345678. Why? Because Code First followed its convention that a Key that is an integer is presumed to be a database identity field and therefore, Entity Framework did not provide the SocialSecurityNumber value in the INSERT command. It let the database generate the value. In fact, if you look at the SocialSecurityNumber value of the person instance after SaveChanges is called, it has been updated to reflect the database-generated value, 1.

To fix this, we need to add some configuration to override the Identity convention, because in this case DatabaseGeneratedOption.Identity is wrong. Instead we want None:

```
    [Key, DatabaseGenerated(DatabaseGeneratedOption.None)]
    public int SocialSecurityNumber { get; set; }
```

Then, running the app again, you can see in Figure 3-6 that the value provided by the application was inserted into the database as expected.

	SocialSecurityNumber	FirstName	LastName
1	12345678	Rowan	Miller

Figure 3-6. SocialSecurityNumber value inserted by EF

`DatabaseGeneratedOption.Computed` is used to specify a mapping to a database field that is computed. For example, if there was a `FullName` field in the `People` table with a formula that combined the values of `FirstName` and `LastName`, you would want to let Entity Framework know so that it would not attempt to save data into that column.

You cannot specify the formula to use for a computed column in Code First and, therefore, you can only use `Computed` when mapping to an existing database. Otherwise, the database provider will throw a runtime exception when it encounters the `Computed` configuration while trying to create the database.

Configuring Database-Generated Options with the Fluent API

The `DatabaseGeneratedOption` can be configured on a particular property. You can append this configuration to the `HasKey` you applied earlier, for example:

```
modelBuilder.Entity<Trip>()
  .HasKey(t => t.Identifier)
  .Property(t => t.Identifier)
  .HasDatabaseGeneratedOption(DatabaseGeneratedOption.Identity);
```

Or you can create a separate statement:

```
modelBuilder.Entity<Person>()
  .HasKey(p => t.SocialSecurityNumber);
modelBuilder.Entity<Person>()
  .Property(p => p.SocialSecurityNumber)
  .HasDatabaseGeneratedOption(DatabaseGeneratedOption.None);
```

You'll notice that the `DatabaseGeneratedOption` enums are within the `System.ComponentModel.DataAnnotations` namespace in *EntityFramework.dll*. You'll also need to have a using statement for this namespace at the top of the context class file.

Configuring TimeStamp/RowVersion Fields for Optimistic Concurrency

Convention	None
Data Annotation	TimeStamp
Fluent	Entity<T>.Property(t=>t.*PropertyName*).IsRowVersion()

Entity Framework has supported *optimistic concurrency* since the first version. Chapter 23 of the second edition of *Programming Entity Framework* covers optimistic concurrency in depth. Here we'll show you how to configure your classes to map to RowVersion (also known as TimeStamp) fields and at the same time instruct Entity Framework to use these fields for concurrency checking when performing updates or deletes on the database.

With Code First you can flag a field to be used in optimistic concurrency checks regardless of what type it maps to in the database, or you can take it a step further and specify that the concurrency field maps to a TimeStamp field.

Only one property in a class can be configured as a TimeStamp property.

 RowVersion and TimeStamp are two terms for the same data type. SQL Server has always used TimeStamp, while many other databases use the more aptly named RowVersion. As of SQL Server 2008, the timestamp data type was changed to be called rowversion, but most of the tools (e.g., SQL Server Management Studio, Visual Studio) continue to display this as timestamp.

Code First Convention and TimeStamp fields

By default, Code First does not recognize TimeStamp properties, so there is no conventional behavior. You must configure properties to get the behavior.

Using Data Annotations to Configure TimeStamp

Not just any property can be mapped to a timestamp database type. You must use a byte array. With that, the Data Annotation is simple: TimeStamp.

Add the following property to both the Trip and Person classes:

```
[Timestamp]
public byte[] RowVersion { get; set; }
```

Then run the console app again, ensuring that both the InsertTrip and InsertPerson methods are called from the Main method.

In the database you'll see that the new RowVersion column (Figure 3-7) has been added to both tables and its type is a non-nullable timestamp.

The database will automatically create a new value for these fields any time the row is modified. But TimeStamp doesn't only affect the database mapping. It also causes the properties to be seen by Entity Framework as concurrency tokens. If you have worked with an EDMX file, this is the equivalent of setting the property's ConcurrencyMode to Fixed. Any time Entity Framework performs an insert, update, or delete to the database, it will take the concurrency field into account, returning the updated database value on every INSERT and UPDATE and passing in the original value from the property with every UPDATE and DELETE.

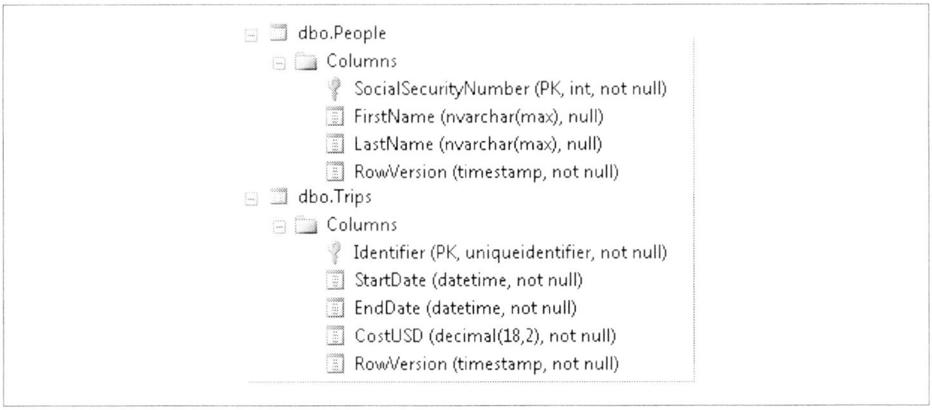

Figure 3-7. People and Trips with RowVersion timestamp fields

For example, Example 3-8 shows the SQL that was sent to the database when Save Changes was called in the InsertPerson method:

Example 3-8. INSERT combined with SELECT to return new RowVersion

```
exec sp_executesql N
'insert [dbo].[People]([SocialSecurityNumber], [FirstName], [LastName])
values (@0, @1, @2)
select [RowVersion]
from [dbo].[People]
where @@ROWCOUNT > 0 and [SocialSecurityNumber] = @0',
N'@0 int,@1 nvarchar(max) ,@2 nvarchar(max) ',@0=12345678,@1=N'Rowan',@2=N'Miller'
```

Not only does Entity Framework tell the database to perform the INSERT, but it also requests the RowVersion value back. EF will always do this with a property that is flagged for concurrency, even if it is not a timestamp value.

Even more critical are the UPDATE and DELETE commands, because here is where the concurrency check occurs.

We've added a new method to the app, UpdatePerson, shown in Example 3-9.

Example 3-9. The UpdateTrip method

```
private static void UpdateTrip()
{
  using (var context = new BreakAwayContext())
  {
    var trip = context.Trips.FirstOrDefault();
    trip.CostUSD = 750;
    context.SaveChanges();
  }
}
```

Example 3-10 shows the SQL executed when SaveChanges is called in the UpdateTrip method.

Example 3-10. UPDATE that filters on original RowVersion and returns new RowVersion

```
exec sp_executesql N'update [dbo].[Trips]
set [CostUSD] = @0
where (([Identifier] = @1) and ([RowVersion] = @2))
select [RowVersion]
from [dbo].[Trips]
where @@ROWCOUNT > 0 and [Identifier] = @1',
N'@0 decimal(18,2),@1 uniqueidentifier,@2 binary(8)',
@0=750.00,@1='D1086EFE-5C5B-405D-9F09-688981BB5B41',@2=0x0000000000001773
```

Notice the where predicate used to locate the trip being updated—it filters on the Identifier and the RowVersion. If someone else has modified the trip since it was retrieved by our method, the RowVersion will have changed and there will be no row that matches the filter. The UPDATE will fail and Entity Framework will throw an Optimistic ConcurrencyException.

Configuring TimeStamp/RowVersion with Fluent API

While the Data Annotation uses the term TimeStamp, the Fluent configuration uses the term RowVersion. To specify a RowVersion property, append the IsRowVersion() method to the Property.

With DbModelBuilder, you configure the Property like this:

```
modelBuilder.Entity<Person>()
    .Property(p => p.RowVersion).IsRowVersion();
```

Inside an EntityTypeConfiguration<T> class the configuration looks like:

```
Property(p => p.RowVersion).IsRowVersion();
```

Configuring Non-Timestamp Fields for Concurrency

Convention	None
Data Annotation	ConcurrencyCheck
Fluent	Entity<T>.Property(t=>t.*PropertyName*).IsConcurrencyToken()

A less common way to provide concurrency checking involves fields that are not row versioning types. For example, some databases do not even have a row version type. So though you won't be able to specifically configure a row version property, you may still want the concurrency checking on one or more database fields.

The Person class currently uses the property SocialSecurityNumber as its identity key. Perhaps the class used a PersonId property for its identity key and SocialSecurityNum ber was simply an integer property not used for identity tracking. In that case, you might want to have a way to avoid conflicts in case the SocialSecurityNumber is changed, because in the United States (not taking illegal activity into account) a social security number uniquely identifies a citizen. Therefore, if a user is editing a Person record, perhaps changing the spelling of the FirstName, but in the meantime, someone else changes that person's Social Security Number, the user changing the FirstName should be alerted of a conflict when she attempts to save her changes. Flagging the SocialSe curityNumber property as a concurrency checking field will provide this check.

Configuring for Optimistic Concurrency with Data Annotations

Example 3-11 shows the modified class with the SocialSecurityNumber configured with the ConcurrencyCheck annotation.

Example 3-11. Modified Person class with a ConcurrencyCheck

```
public class Person
{
  public int PersonId { get; set; }
  [ConcurrencyCheck]
  public int SocialSecurityNumber { get; set; }
  public string FirstName { get; set; }
  public string LastName { get; set; }
}
```

Example 3-12 shows a new method to force an update to a Person. If you call this method, you will need to call InsertPerson first to ensure there is an existing Person in the database.

Example 3-12. The UpdatePerson method

```
private static void UpdatePerson()
{
  using (var context = new BreakAwayContext())
  {
    var person = context.People.FirstOrDefault();
    person.FirstName = "Rowena";
    context.SaveChanges();
  }
}
```

Just as you saw with the Trip.RowVersion field in Example 3-10, when an update or delete is sent to the database, the SQL (shown in Example 3-13) looks for the row with not only the matching key (PersonId) but also with the concurrency field (SocialSecur ityNumber) that matches the originally retrieved value.

Example 3-13. SQL providing concurrency checking on SocialSecurityNumber

```
exec sp_executesql N'update [dbo].[People]
set [FirstName] = @0
where (([PersonId] = @1) and ([SocialSecurityNumber] = @2))
',N'@0 nvarchar(max) ,@1 int,@2 int',@0=N'Rowena',@1=1,@2=12345678
```

If no match is found (meaning that the SocialSecurityNumber has changed in the database), the update will fail and an OptimisticConcurrencyException will be thrown.

Configuring for Optimistic Concurrency with Fluent API

The Fluent API method for concurrency is IsConcurrencyToken and gets applied to a Property as shown in Example 3-14.

Example 3-14. Configuring concurrency checking fluently

```
public class PersonConfiguration : EntityTypeConfiguration<Person>
{
  public PersonConfiguration()
  {
    Property(p => p.SocialSecurityNumber).IsConcurrencyToken();
  }
}
```

We've decided it's time for Person to have its own configuration class, so the configuration is inside this new class. Don't forget to add the PersonConfiguration to the modelBuilder.Configurations collection in your OnModelCreating method.

Mapping to Non-Unicode Database Types

Convention	All strings map to Unicode-encoded database types
Data Annotation	*unavailable*
Fluent	Entity<T>.Property(t=>t.*PropertyName*).IsUnicode(*boolean*)

By default, Code First convention presumes that all strings map to Unicode string types in a database.

There is no Data Annotation for mapping Unicode.

See Dane Morgridge's blog post "EF4 Code First Control Unicode and Decimal Precision, Scale with Attributes (*http://geekswithblogs.net/dane morgridge/archive/2010/12/20/ef4-code-first-control-unicode-and-deci mal-precision-scale-with.aspx*)," which discusses getting around this limitation.

You can specify whether or not a string maps to a Unicode string type in the database with the IsUnicode method. The following code added to the LodgingConfiguration tells Code First to not map the Owner property as a Unicode encoded type:

```
Property(l => l.Owner).IsUnicode(false);
```

Affecting the Precision and Scale of Decimals

Convention	Decimals are 18, 2
Data Annotation	*unavailable*
Fluent	Entity<T>.Property(t=>t.*PropertyName*).HasPrecision(n,n)

Precision (the number of digits in a number) and Scale (the number of digits to the right of the decimal point in a number) are property attributes that can be configured with the Fluent API, though not with Data Annotations.

To see how it works, we'll add a new decimal property to the Lodging class: MilesFrom NearestAirport:

```
public decimal MilesFromNearestAirport { get; set; }
```

Convention for Precision and Scale

By default, Decimal types have a Precision of 18 and a Scale of 2, as shown in Figure 3-8.

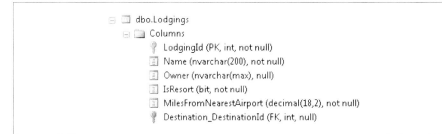

Figure 3-8. Decimal property default Precision and Scale

Data Annotations for Precision and Scale

Precision and Scale cannot be configured with Data Annotations.

Fluent Configuration for Precision and Scale

With the Fluent API, you configure both the precision and scale with a single method, HasPrecision. Even if one of the defaults is correct, you need to include both:

```
Property(l => l.MilesFromNearestAirport).HasPrecision(8, 1);
```

As a result, Figure 3-9 shows the `MilesFromNearestAirport` database column with the specified precision.

Figure 3-9. MilesFromNearestAirport with its configured precision

Working with Complex Types in Code First

Entity Framework has supported using *complex types* since the first version. Complex types are also known as *value types* and can be used to add additional properties to another class. What differentiates complex types from entity types is that a complex type does not have its own key. It is dependent on its "host" type for change tracking and persistence.

A type that has no key property and is used as a property in one or more mapped types will be recognized by Code First convention as a complex type. Code First will presume that the properties of the complex type are contained in the table to which the host type maps.

What if the People table in an existing database included properties to represent a person's address? A class that mapped directly to that table might look like the Person class in Example 3-15.

Example 3-15. Individual properties representing an address in Person

```
public class Person
{
  public int PersonId { get; set; }
  public int SocialSecurityNumber { get; set; }
  public string FirstName { get; set; }
  public string LastName { get; set; }
  public string StreetAddress { get; set; }
  public string City { get; set; }
  public string State { get; set; }
  public string ZipCode { get; set; }
}
```

But in your model you prefer to have `Address` as a separate class and be simply a value type property of `Person`, as shown in Example 3-16.

Example 3-16. Address type as a property of Person

```
public class Address
{
  public int AddressId { get; set; }
  public string StreetAddress { get; set; }
  public string City { get; set; }
  public string State { get; set; }
  public string ZipCode { get; set; }
}
public class Person
{
  public int PersonId { get; set; }
  public int SocialSecurityNumber { get; set; }
  public string FirstName { get; set; }
  public string LastName { get; set; }
  public Address Address { get; set; }
}
```

By convention this setup would result in a separate table, `Addresses`, for the `Address` data. But the goal is to have the properties of `Address` be fields of the `People` table.

You can achieve this if `Address` is a complex type. And if you have other tables that also contain these same properties, you can use the `Address` complex type in their classes as well.

 Remember that by definition, a complex type does not have a key property.

Defining Complex Types by Convention

The conventional way to turn the `Address` class into a complex type is to remove the `AddressId` property. Let's comment that out for now:

```
// public int AddressId { get; set; }
```

Before rerunning the application, you'll need to consider the `InsertPerson` method listed in Example 3-7 before `Address` even existed. Because the `Address` property is not handled and will therefore be null, it will cause a `DbUpdateException` to be thrown by `SaveChanges`. Rather than worry about that in any code that inserts a new `Person`, you can instantiate a new `Address` in the constructor of the `Person` class (Example 3-17).

Example 3-17. Instantiating the Address property in the constructor of the Person class

```
public class Person
{
  public Person()
  {
    Address = new Address();
```

```
    }
. . .
```

In addition to the rule that a complex type does not have a key, Code First has two other rules that must be satisfied for detecting complex types. The complex type can only contain primitive properties and, when used in another class, it can only be used as a non-collection type. In other words, if you want a property in the `Person` class that is a `List<Address>` or some other type that results in a collection of `Address` types, `Address` cannot be a complex type.

Conventional Complex Type Rules

1. Complex types have no key property.
2. Complex types can only contain primitive properties.
3. When used as a property in another class, the property must represent a single instance. It cannot be a collection type.

After running the application, Figure 3-10 shows that the `Address` fields are part of the `People` table. The Code First convention recognized that `Address` was meant to be a complex type and responded in the new model that it generated.

```
⊟ 🗍 DataAccess.BreakAwayContext
  ⊞ 🗀 Database Diagrams
  ⊟ 🗀 Tables
    ⊞ 🗀 System Tables
    ⊞ 🗔 dbo.Destinations
    ⊞ 🗔 dbo.EdmMetadata
    ⊞ 🗔 dbo.Lodgings
    ⊟ 🗔 dbo.People
      ⊟ 🗀 Columns
          🔑 PersonId (PK, int, not null)
          🗔 SocialSecurityNumber (int, not null)
          🗔 FirstName (nvarchar(max), null)
          🗔 LastName (nvarchar(max), null)
          🗔 Address_StreetAddress (nvarchar(max), null)
          🗔 Address_City (nvarchar(max), null)
          🗔 Address_State (nvarchar(max), null)
          🗔 Address_ZipCode (nvarchar(max), null)
      ⊞ 🗀 Keys
      ⊞ 🗀 Constraints
      ⊞ 🗀 Triggers
      ⊞ 🗀 Indexes
      ⊞ 🗀 Statistics
    ⊞ 🗔 dbo.Trips
```

Figure 3-10. Properties of the Address complex type as fields in the People table

Notice how the Address fields are named: HostPropertyName_Property Name, for example. This is the Code First convention. In Chapter 5, you'll learn how to configure column names for complex type properties.

Configuring Unconventional Complex Types

What if your intended complex type, Address, did not follow convention? Perhaps you want to have an AddressId property even though you know that an individual Address instance will not be change-tracked by Entity Framework?.

If we add the AddressId property back into the Address class and rerun the application, Code First convention will not be able to infer your intent and will go back to creating a separate Addresses table that has a PK/FK relationship to the People table.

You can fix this by explicitly configuring the complex type.

Specifying complex types with Data Annotations

There is a ComplexType Data Annotation that you can apply to a class.

Example 3-18. Address with AddressId reinstated and a ComplexType configuration

```
[ComplexType]
public class Address
{
  public int AddressId { get; set; }
  public string StreetAddress { get; set; }
  public string City { get; set; }
  public string State { get; set; }
  public string ZipCode { get; set; }
}
```

With this in place, when you run the application again, the model will be rebuilt and the resulting database schema will once again match Figure 3-10, with the addition of a new int field called Address_AddressId.

Specifying complex types with the Fluent API

To instruct Code First that a type is a complex type using the Fluent API, you must use the DbModelBuilder.ComplexType method.

```
modelBuilder.ComplexType<Address>();
```

Example 3-19 shows the modified OnModelCreating method.

Example 3-19. Specifying a complex type fluently

```
protected override void OnModelCreating(DbModelBuilder modelBuilder)
{
  modelBuilder.Configurations.Add(new DestinationConfiguration());
  modelBuilder.Configurations.Add(new LodgingConfiguration());
```

```
  modelBuilder.Configurations.Add(new PersonConfiguration());
  modelBuilder.Configurations.Add(new TripConfiguration());
  modelBuilder.ComplexType<Address>();
}
```

This modelBuilder configuration is intentionally positioned after the code for adding configurations. *In-line configurations*, those which are called directly against the modelBuilder instance inside the OnModelCreating method, must come after any code that adds configuration classes to the Configurations collection.

Working with More Complicated Complex Types

Recall that one of the conventions for complex types is that the type can only contain primitive types. If your complex type doesn't satisfy this rule, you will have to configure the type. Here is an example.

We've created two new types, PersonalInfo and Measurement, shown in Example 3-20. PersonalInfo contains two Measurement properties. Notice there is no identity property in either type. Our intent is for both PersonalInfo and Measurement to be complex types. The PersonalInfo complex type makes use of the Measurement complex type; this is known as a nested complex type.

Example 3-20. New classes: PersonalInfo and Measurement

```
public class PersonalInfo
{
  public Measurement Weight { get; set; }
  public Measurement Height { get; set; }
  public string DietryRestrictions { get; set; }
}

public class Measurement
{
  public decimal Reading { get; set; }
  public string Units { get; set; }
}
```

We then add the new PersonalInfo property into the Person class:

```
    public PersonalInfo Info { get; set; }
```

We'll also need to add some logic to the constructor of Person to instantiate these new properties:

```
    public Person()
    {
      Address = new Address();
      Info = new PersonalInfo
      {
        Weight = new Measurement(),
        Height = new Measurement()
```

```
    };
  }
```

If you go ahead and run the application, the model builder will throw an exception:

> EntityType 'PersonalInfo' has no key defined. Define the key for this EntityType.

Code First does not recognize that we want `PersonalInfo` to be a complex type. The reason is that we broke one of the rules: *the complex type must contain only primitive types*. There are two `Measurement` properties in `PersonalInfo`. Because those are not primitive types, convention did not see `PersonalInfo` as a complex type.

If you add the `ComplexType` configuration to the `PersonalInfo` class, Code First will be able to properly build the model. You don't need to configure the `Measurement` class since it follows convention for Complex Types.

Configuring Properties of Complex Types

Code First will treat complex type properties in the same way as any other type and you can configure them with Data Annotations or fluently.

Configuring Complex Types with Data Annotations

Recall that Code First convention named them using the pattern `ComplexTypeName_Prop ertyName` (see Figure 3-10). You can apply Data Annotations to complex types just as you use them for the other classes. Example 3-21 uses an annotation you are already familiar with, `MaxLength`, to affect a property in the `Address` type.

Example 3-21. Configuring the StreetAddress property of the Address

```
[ComplexType]
public class Address
{
  public int AddressId { get; set; }
  [MaxLength(150)]
  public string StreetAddress { get; set; }
  public string City { get; set; }
  public string State { get; set; }
  public string ZipCode { get; set; }
}
```

Figure 3-11 shows the `People` table of the database with the modified `Address_Stree tAddress` field. You can also see the `Address_AddressId` field that came from reinstating `AddressId` and the fields added as a result of the `PersonalInfo` complex type and its `Measurement` subtype.

```
⊟ ☐ dbo.People
  ⊟ ☐ Columns
      🔑 PersonId (PK, int, not null)
      ▦ SocialSecurityNumber (int, not null)
      ▦ FirstName (nvarchar(max), null)
      ▦ LastName (nvarchar(max), null)
      ▦ Info_Weight_Reading (decimal(18,2), not null)
      ▦ Info_Weight_Units (nvarchar(max), null)
      ▦ Info_Height_Reading (decimal(18,2), not null)
      ▦ Info_Height_Units (nvarchar(max), null)
      ▦ Info_DietryRestrictions (nvarchar(max), null)
      ▦ Address_AddressId (int, not null)
      ▦ Address_StreetAddress (nvarchar(150), null)
      ▦ Address_City (nvarchar(max), null)
      ▦ Address_State (nvarchar(max), null)
      ▦ Address_ZipCode (nvarchar(max), null)
```

Figure 3-11. Address_StreetAddress field after MaxLength(150) configuration applied

 In Chapter 5, we'll revisit the column names of this complex type and fix them up when you learn about configuring column names.

Configuring Complex Type Properties with the Fluent API

There are two ways to configure properties of complex types with the Fluent API. You can start with the host entity or you can start with the complex type itself. According to the Entity Framework team, the latter is the preferred way to configure property attributes. `MaxLength` falls into this category. When we get to the examples of configuring column names in Chapter 5, we'll configure from the `Person` entity since the goal will be to impact how the `Person` mapping handles the naming of its fields.

The model builder recognizes the difference between complex types and entity types.

If you want to configure directly from the `DbModelBuilder`, you must begin with its `Complex<T>` method, instead of the `Entity<T>` method you've used so far. Example 3-22 demonstrates configuring a Complex Type directly from the `modelBuilder` instance in `OnCreatingModel`.

Example 3-22. Configuring a property of the Address complex type

```
modelBuilder.ComplexType<Address>()
  .Property(p => p.StreetAddress).HasMaxLength(150);
```

If you prefer to encapsulate your configurations, you'll need to inherit from `ComplexTypeConfiguration` class rather than `EntityTypeConfiguration`, as shown in Example 3-23.

Example 3-23. Configuring the length of StreetAddress in the Address ComplexType

```
public class AddressConfiguration :
 ComplexTypeConfiguration<Address>
{
  public AddressConfiguration()
  {
    Property(a => a.StreetAddress).HasMaxLength(150);
  }
}
```

You'll also need to be sure that the you add this AddressConfiguration to the model:

```
modelBuilder.Configurations.Add(new AddressConfiguration());
```

Summary

In this chapter you've seen many of the presumptions that Code First makes about what the model should look like based on what it sees in your classes. Strings become nvarchar(max) in SQL Server. Numbers acquire a precision that lets them have up to 18 digits (which will enable you to keep track of values in the quadrillions!) and 2 decimal places. While these and other defaults may be useful for very generic scenarios, you do have the ability to apply configurations to specify the sizes you prefer. You've also learned how to ensure that Entity Framework is aware that values should be treated as timestamps or at least concurrency fields. You've also worked with properties that point to complex types—types that do not have keys and can only be tracked when they are a property of another class that is tracked.

Code First conventions take care of a good portion of common scenarios, but it is the ability to override these conventions with your own configurations that affords you great control over how your classes are managed by Entity Framework.

CHAPTER 4

Using Convention and Configuration for Relationships

In Chapter 3, you learned about convention and configuration that affect attributes of properties and the effects that these have on the database. In this chapter, the focus will be on convention and configuration that affects the relationships between classes. This includes how classes relate to one another in memory, as well as the corresponding foreign key constraints in the database. You'll learn about controlling multiplicity, whether or not a relationship is required, and working with cascade deletes. You'll see the conventional behavior and learn how to control the relationships using Data Annotations and the Fluent API.

You'll start seeing more configuration that can be performed with the Fluent API but cannot be done through Data Annotations. Recall, however, that if you really love to apply configuration with attributes, the note in "Mapping to Non-Unicode Database Types" on page 51 points to a blog post that demonstrates how to create attributes to perform configuration that is only available through the Fluent API.

You've already seen some of the relationship conventions in action throughout the earlier chapters of this book. You built a `Destination` class (Example 4-1) that has a `Lodgings` property which is a `List<Lodging>`.

Example 4-1. The Destination class with a property that points to the Lodging class

```
public class Destination
{
  public int DestinationId { get; set; }
  public string Name { get; set; }
  public string Country { get; set; }
  public string Description { get; set; }
  public byte[] Photo { get; set; }

  public List<Lodging> Lodgings { get; set; }
}
```

On the other end of the relationship, the `Lodging` class (Example 4-2) has a `Destina tion` property that represents a single `Destination` instance.

Example 4-2. The Lodging class with its reference back to the Destination class

```
public class Lodging
{
  public int LodgingId { get; set; }
  public string Name { get; set; }
  public string Owner { get; set; }
  public bool IsResort { get; set; }
  public decimal MilesFromNearestAirport { get; set; }

  public Destination Destination { get; set; }
}
```

Code First sees that you have defined both a reference and a collection navigation property, so by convention it will configure this as a one-to-many relationship. Based on this, Code First can also determine that `Lodging` is the dependent end of the relationship (the end with the foreign key) and `Destination` is the principal end (the end with the primary key). It therefore knows that the table `Lodging` maps to will need a foreign key pointing back to the primary key of `Destination`. You saw this played out in Chapter 2, where it created the `Destination_DestinationId` foreign key field in the `Lodgings` table.

In the rest of this chapter, you will get an understanding of the full set of conventions that Code First has around relationships and how to override those conventions when they don't align with your intent.

Relationships in Your Application Logic

Once Code First has worked out the model and its relationships, Entity Framework will treat those relationships just the same as it does with POCOs that are mapped using an EDMX file. All of the rules you learned about working with POCO objects throughout *Programming Entity Framework* still apply. For example, if you have a foreign key property and a navigation property, Entity Framework will keep them in sync. If you have bidirectional relationships, Entity Framework will keep them in sync as well. At what point Entity Framework synchronizes the values is determined by whether you are leveraging dynamic proxies. Without the proxies, Entity Framework relies on an implicit or explicit call to `DetectChanges`. With the proxies, the synchronization happens in response to the property value being changed. Typically you do not need to worry about calling `DetectChanges` because `DbContext` will take care of calling it for you when you call any of its methods that rely on things being in sync. The Entity Framework team recommends that you only use dynamic proxies if you find a need to; typically this would be around performance tuning. POCO classes without proxies are usually simpler to interact with, as you don't need to be aware of the additional behaviors and nuances that are associated with proxies.

Working with Multiplicity

As you've seen, Code First will create relationships when it sees navigation properties and, optionally, foreign key properties. Details about those navigation properties and foreign keys will help the conventions determine *multiplicity* of each end. We'll focus on foreign keys a little later in this chapter; for now, let's take a look at relationships where there is no foreign key property defined in your class.

Code First applies a set of rules to work out the multiplicity of each relationship. The rules use the navigation properties you defined in your classes to determine multiplicity. There can either be a pair of navigation properties that point to each other (bidirectional relationship) or a single navigation property (unidirectional relationship):

- If your classes contain a reference and a collection navigation property, Code First assumes a one-to-many relationship.
- Code First will also assume a one-to-many relationship if your classes include a navigation property on only one side of the relationship (i.e., either the collection or the reference, but not both).
- If your classes include two collection properties, Code First will use a many-to-many relationship by default.
- If your classes include two reference properties, Code First will assume a one-to-one relationship.
- In the case of one-to-one relationships, you will need to provide some additional information so that Code First knows which entity is the principal and which is the dependent. You'll see this in action a little later on in this chapter, in the "Working with One-to-One Relationships" on page 84 section. If no foreign key property is defined in your classes, Code First will assume the relationship is optional (i.e., the one end of the relationship is actually zero-or-one as opposed to exactly-one).
- In the "Working with Foreign Keys" on page 66 section of this chapter, you will see that when you define a foreign key property in your classes, Code First uses the nullability of that property to determine if the relationship is required or optional.

Looking back at the `Lodging` to `Destination` relationship that we just revisited, you can see these rules in action. Having a collection and a reference property meant that Code First assumed it was a one-to-many relationship. We can also see that, by convention, Code First has configured it as an optional relationship. But in our scenario it really doesn't make sense to have a `Lodging` that doesn't belong to a `Destination`. So let's take a look at how we can make this a required relationship.

Configuring Multiplicity with Data Annotations

Most of the multiplicity configuration needs to be done using the Fluent API. But we can use Data Annotations to specify that a relationship is required. This is as simple as placing the Required annotation on the reference property that you want to be required. Modify Lodging by adding the Required annotation to the Destination property (Example 4-3).

Example 4-3. Required annotation added to Destination property

```
public class Lodging
{
  public int LodgingId { get; set; }
  public string Name { get; set; }
  public string Owner { get; set; }
  public bool IsResort { get; set; }
  public decimal MilesFromNearestAirport { get; set; }

  [Required]
  public Destination Destination { get; set; }
}
```

If you were to run the application so that the database gets recreated with the change you just made, you would see that the Destination_DestinationId column in the Lodgings table no longer allows null values (Figure 4-1). This is because the relationship is now required.

Figure 4-1. Lodgings table with required foreign key

Configuring Multiplicity with the Fluent API

Configuring relationships with the Fluent API can look confusing if you haven't taken the time to understand the fundamental ideas. We'll lead you down the path to enlightenment.

When fixing relationships with Data Annotations, you apply annotations directly to the navigation properties. It's very different with the Fluent API, where you are literally configuring the relationship, not a property. In order to do so, you must first identify the relationship. Sometimes it's enough to mention one end, but most often you need to describe the complete relationship.

To identify a relationship, you point to its navigation properties. Regardless of which end you begin with, this is the pattern:

```
Entity.Has[Multiplicity](Property).With[Multiplicity](Property)
```

The multiplicity can be Optional (a property that can have a single instance or be null), Required (a property that must have a single instance), or Many (a property with a collection of a single type).

The Has methods are as follows:

- HasOptional
- HasRequired
- HasMany

In most cases you will follow the Has method with one of the following With methods:

- WithOptional
- WithRequired
- WithMany

Example 4-4 shows a concrete example using the existing one-to-many relationship between Destination and Lodging. This configuration doesn't really do anything, because it is configuring exactly what Code First detected by convention. Later in this chapter, you will see that this approach is used to identify a relationship so that you can perform further configuration related to foreign keys and cascade delete.

Example 4-4. Specifying an optional one-to-many relationship

```
modelBuilder.Entity<Destination>()
  .HasMany(d => d.Lodgings)
  .WithOptional(l => l.Destination);
```

Example 4-5 shows what this same configuration would look like inside an EntityTypeConfiguration class rather than directly inside OnModelCreating.

Example 4-5. Specifying a relationship in an EntityConfiguration class

```
HasMany(d => d.Lodgings)
  .WithOptional(l => l.Destination);
```

This identifies a relationship that Destination Has. It has a Many relationship that is defined by its property, Lodgings. And the Lodgings end of the relationship comes along With a relationship (which is Optional) to Destination. Figure 4-2 attempts to help you visualize this relationship the way the model builder sees it.

We looked at how to change this to be a required relationship with Data Annotations, so now let's see how to do the same with the Fluent API. Add the configuration shown in Example 4-6 to your DestinationConfiguration class.

Example 4-6. Configuring a required relationship with the Fluent API

```
HasMany(d => d.Lodgings)
  .WithRequired(l => l.Destination);
```

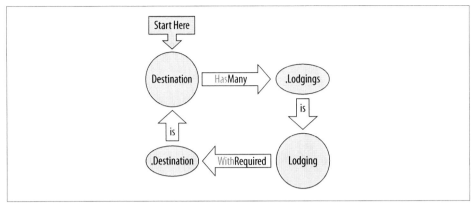

Figure 4-2. How Entity Framework perceives a one- to-many relationship

This looks very similar to the configuration we saw in Example 4-5, except, instead of calling `HasOptional`, you are now calling `HasRequired`. This lets Code First know that you want this one-to-many relationship to be *required* rather than optional. Run the application again and you will see that the database looks the same as it did in Figure 4-1 when you used Data Annotations to configure the relationship to be required.

 If you are configuring a one-to-one relationship where both ends are required or both ends are optional, Code First will need some more information from you to work out which end is the principal and which end is the dependent. This area of the Fluent API can get very confusing! The good news is that you probably won't need to use it very often. This topic is covered in detail in "Working with One-to-One Relationships" on page 84.

Working with Foreign Keys

So far we've just looked at relationships where there isn't a foreign key property in your class. For example, `Lodging` just contains a reference property that points to `Destination`, but there is no property to store the key value of the `Destination` it points to. In these cases, we have seen that Code First will introduce a foreign key in the database for you. But now let's look at what happens when we include the foreign key property in the class itself.

In the previous section you added some configuration to make the `Lodging` to `Destination` relationship required. Go ahead and remove this configuration so that we can observe the Code First conventions in action. With the configuration removed, add a `DestinationId` property into the `Lodging` class:

```
public int DestinationId { get; set; }
```

Once you have added the foreign key property to the Lodging class, go ahead and run your application. The database will get recreated in response to the change you just made. If you inspect the columns of the Lodgings table, you will notice that Code First has automatically detected that DestinationId is a foreign key for the Lodging to Desti nation relationship and is no longer generating the Destination_DestinationId foreign key (Figure 4-3).

Figure 4-3. Lodgings with FK after DestinationId is added to the class

As you might expect by now, Code First has a set or rules it applies to try and locate a foreign key property when it discovers a relationship. The rules are based on the name of the property. The foreign key property will be discovered by convention if it is named *[Target Type Key Name]*, *[Target Type Name]* + *[Target Type Key Name]*, or *[Navigation Property Name]* + *[Target Type Key Name]*. The DestinationId property you added matched the first of these three rules. Name matching is case-insensitive, so you could have named the property DestinationID, DeStInAtIoNiD, or any other variation of casing. If no foreign key is detected, and none is configured, Code First falls back to automatically introducing one in the database.

Why Foreign Key Properties?

It's common when coding to want to identify a relationship with another class. For example, you may be creating a new Lodging and want to specify which Destination the Lodging is associated with. If the particular destination is in memory, you can set the relationship through the navigation property:

```
myLodging.Destination=myDestinationInstance;
```

However, if the destination is not in memory, this would require you to first execute a query on the database to retrieve that destination so that you can set the property. There are times when you may not have the object in memory, but you do have access to that object's key value. With a foreign key property, you can simply use the key value without depending on having that instance in memory:

```
myLodging.DestinationId=3;
```

Additionally, in the specific case when the Lodging is new and you attach the preexisting Destination instance, there are scenarios where Entity Framework will set the

Destination's state to Added even though it already exists in the database. If you are only working with the foreign key, you can avoid this problem.

There's something else interesting that happens when you add the foreign key property. Without the DestinationId foreign key property, Code First convention allowed Lodging.Destination to be optional, meaning you could add a Lodging without a Destination. If you check back to Figure 2-1 in Chapter 2, you'll see that the Destination_DestinationId field in the Lodgings table is nullable. Now with the addition of the DestinationId property, the database field is no longer nullable and you'll find that you can no longer save a Lodging that has neither the Destination nor DestinationId property populated. This is because DestinationId is of type int, which is a value type and cannot be assigned null. If DestinationId was of type Nullable<int>, the relationship would remain optional. By convention, Code First is using the nullability of the foreign key property in your class to determine if the relationship is required or optional.

It's Just Easier with Foreign Key Properties

Code First allows you define relationships without using foreign key properties in your classes. However, some of the confusing behaviors that developers encounter when working with related data in Entity Framework stems from dependent classes that do not have a foreign key property. The Entity Framework has certain rules that it follows when it checks relationship constraints, performs inserts, etc. When there's no foreign key property to keep track of a required principal (e.g., knowing what the destination is for a particular lodging), it's up to the developer to ensure that you've somehow provided the required information to EF. You can also learn more in Julie's January 2012 Data Points column, "Making Do with Absent Foreign Keys" (*http://msdn.com/magazine*).

Specifying Unconventionally Named Foreign Keys

What happens when you have a foreign key, but it doesn't follow Code First convention?

Let's introduce a new InternetSpecial class that allows us to keep track of special pricing for the various lodgings (Example 4-7). This class has both a navigation property (Accommodation) and a foreign key property (AccommodationId) for the same relationship.

Example 4-7. The new InternetSpecial class

```
using System;
namespace Model
{
  public class InternetSpecial
  {
    public int InternetSpecialId { get; set; }
    public int Nights { get; set; }
```

```
    public decimal CostUSD { get; set; }
    public DateTime FromDate { get; set; }
    public DateTime ToDate { get; set; }

    public int AccommodationId { get; set; }
    public Lodging Accommodation { get; set; }
  }
}
```

Lodging will need a new property to contain each lodging's special prices:

```
    public List<InternetSpecial> InternetSpecials { get; set; }
```

Code First can see that Lodging has many InternetSpecials and that InternetSpe cials has a Lodging (called Accommodation). Even though there's no DbSet<InternetSpe cial>, InternetSpecial is reachable from Lodging and will therefore be included in the model.

 You'll learn more about how the model builder finds or ignores entities in Chapter 5.

When you run your application again, it will create the table shown in Figure 4-4. Not only is there an AccommodationId column, which is not a foreign key, but there is also another column there which *is* a foreign key, Accommodation_LodgingId.

Figure 4-4. InternetSpecials appears to have two foreign keys

You've seen Code First introduce a foreign key in the database before. As early as Chapter 2, you witnessed the Destination_DestinationId field added to the Lodgings table because Code First detected a need for a foreign key. It's done the same here. Thanks to the Accommodation navigation property, Code First detected a relationship to Lodging and created the Accommodation_LodgingId field using its conventional pat tern. Code First convention was not able to infer that AccommodationId is meant to be the foreign key. It simply found no properties that matched any of the three patterns that Code First convention uses to detect foreign key properties, and therefore created its own foreign key.

Fixing foreign key with Data Annotations

You can configure foreign key properties using the ForeignKey annotation to clarify your intention to Code First. Adding ForeignKey to the AccommodationId, along with information telling it which navigation property represents the relationship it is a foreign key for, will fix the problem:

```
[ForeignKey("Accommodation")]
public int AccommodationId { get; set; }
public Lodging Accommodation { get; set; }
```

Alternatively, you can apply the ForeignKey annotation to the navigation property and tell it which property is the foreign key for the relationship:

```
public int AccommodationId { get; set; }
[ForeignKey("AccommodationId")]
public Lodging Accommodation { get; set; }
```

Which one you use is a matter of personal preference. Either way, you'll end up with the correct foreign key in the database: AccommodationId, as is shown in Figure 4-5.

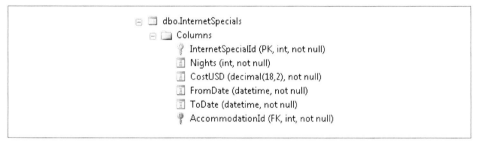

Figure 4-5. AccommodationId correctly identified as the foreign key

Fixing foreign key with the Fluent API

The Fluent API doesn't provide a simple way to configure the property as a foreign key. You'll use the relationship API to configure the correct foreign key. And you can't simply configure that piece of the relationship; you'll need to first specify which relationship you want to configure (as you learned how to do earlier in this chapter) and then apply the fix.

To specify the relationship, begin with the InternetSpecial entity. We'll do that directly from the modelBuilder, although you can certainly create an EntityTypeConfiguration class for InternetSpecial.

In this case, we'll be identifying the relationship but not changing the multiplicity that Code First selected by convention. Example 4-8 specifies the existing relationship.

Example 4-8. Identifying the relationship to be configured

```
modelBuilder.Entity<InternetSpecial>()
  .HasRequired(s => s.Accommodation)
  .WithMany(l => l.InternetSpecials)
```

What we want to change, however, is something about the foreign key that is also involved with this relationship. Code First expects the foreign key property to be named `LodgingId` or one of the other conventional names. So we need to tell it which property truly is the foreign key—`AccommodationId`. Example 4-9 shows adding the `HasForeign Key` method to the relationship you specified in Example 4-8.

Example 4-9. Specifying a foreign key property when it has an unconventional name

```
modelBuilder.Entity<InternetSpecial>()
  .HasRequired(s => s.Accommodation)
  .WithMany(l => l.InternetSpecials)
  .HasForeignKey(s => s.AccommodationId);
```

This, too, will result in the database schema shown in Figure 4-5.

Working with Inverse Navigation Properties

So far Code First has always been able to work out that the two navigation properties we have defined on each end of a relationship are in fact different ends of the same relationship. It has been able to do this because there has only ever been one possible match. For example, `Lodging` only contains a single property that refers to `Destina tion` (`Lodging.Destination`); likewise, `Destination` only contains a single property that references `Lodging` (`Destination.Lodgings`).

While it isn't terribly common, you may run into a scenario where there are multiple relationships between entities. In these cases, Code First won't be able to work out which navigation properties match up. You will need to provide some additional configuration.

For example, what if you kept track of two contacts for each lodging? That would require a `PrimaryContact` and `SecondaryContact` property in the `Lodging` class. Go ahead and add these properties to the `Lodging` class:

```
public Person PrimaryContact { get; set; }
public Person SecondaryContact { get; set; }
```

Let's also introduce the navigation properties on the other end of the relationship. This will allow you to navigate from a `Person` to the `Lodging` instances that they are primary and secondary contact for. Add the following two properties to the `Person` class:

```
public List<Lodging> PrimaryContactFor { get; set; }
public List<Lodging> SecondaryContactFor { get; set; }
```

Code First conventions will make the wrong assumptions about these new relationships you have just added. Because there are two sets of navigation properties, Code First is unable to work out how they match up. When Code First can't be sure which navigation properties are the inverse of each other, it will create a separate relationship for each property. Figure 4-6 shows that Code First is creating four relationships based on the four navigation properties you just added.

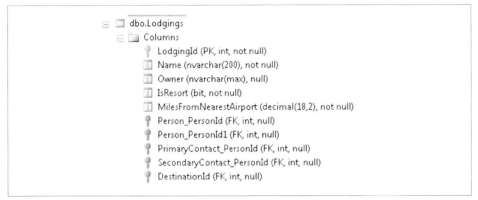

Figure 4-6. Too many foreign keys in the Lodgings table

Code First convention can identify bidirectional relationships, but not when there are multiple bidirectional relationships between two entities. The reason that there are extra foreign keys in Figure 4-6 is that Code First was unable to determine which of the two properties in Lodging that return a Person link up to the List<Lodging> properties in the Person class.

You can add configuration (using Data Annotations or the Fluent API) to present this information to the model builder. With Data Annotations, you'll use an annotation called InverseProperty. With the Fluent API, you'll use a combination of the Has/With methods to specify the correct ends of these relationships.

You can place the annotations on either end of the relationship (or both ends if you want). We'll stick them on the navigation properties in the Lodging class (Example 4-10). The InverseProperty Data Annotation needs the name of the corresponding navigation property in the related class as its parameter.

Example 4-10. Configuring multiple bidirectional relationships from Lodging to Person

```
[InverseProperty("PrimaryContactFor")]
public Person PrimaryContact { get; set; }
[InverseProperty("SecondaryContactFor")]
public Person SecondaryContact { get; set; }
```

With the Fluent API, you need to use the Has/With pattern that you learned about earlier to identify the ends of each relationship. The first configuration in Example 4-11 describes the relationship with Lodging.PrimaryContact on one end and Person.Primary ContactFor on the other. The second configuration is for the relationship between SecondaryContact and SecondaryContactFor.

Example 4-11. Configuring multiple relationships fluently

```
modelBuilder.Entity<Lodging>()
  .HasOptional(l => l.PrimaryContact)
  .WithMany(p => p.PrimaryContactFor);

modelBuilder.Entity< Lodging >()
  .HasOptional(l => l.SecondaryContact)
  .WithMany(p => p.SecondaryContactFor);
```

Working with Cascade Delete

Cascade delete allows dependent data to be automatically deleted when the principal record is deleted. If you delete a Destination, for example, the related Lodgings will also be deleted automatically. Entity Framework supports cascade delete behavior for in-memory data as well as in the database. As discussed in Chapter 19 of the second edition of *Programming Entity Framework*, it is recommended that you implement cascade delete on entities in the model if their mapped database objects also have cascade delete defined.

By convention, Code First switches on cascade delete for required relationships. When a cascade delete is defined, Code First will also configure a cascade delete in the database that it creates. Earlier in this chapter we looked at making the Lodging to Destination relationship required. In other words, a Lodging cannot exist without a Destination. Therefore, if a Destination is deleted, any related Lodgings (that are in memory and being change-tracked by the context) will also be deleted. When SaveChanges is called, the database will delete any related rows that remain in the Lodgings table, using its cascade delete behavior.

Looking at the database, you can see that Code First carried through the cascade delete and set up a constraint on the relationship in the database. Notice the Delete Rule in Figure 4-7 is set to Cascade.

Example 4-12 shows a new method called DeleteDestinationInMemoryAndDbCascade, which we'll use to demonstrate the in-memory and database cascade delete.

The code uses a context to insert a new Destination with a couple of Lodgings. It then saves these Lodgings to the database and records the primary of the new Destination. In a separate context, the code then retrieves the Destination and its related Lodgings, and then uses the Remove method to mark the Destination instance as Deleted. We use Console.WriteLine to inspect the state of one of the related Lodging instances that are in memory. We'll do this using the Entry method of DbContext. The Entry method gives us access to the information that EF has about the state of a given object. Next, the call to SaveChanges persists the deletions to the database.

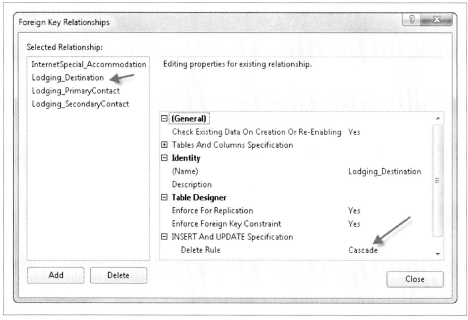

Figure 4-7. Cascade delete defined in a database constraint

Example 4-12. A method to explore cascade deletes

```
private static void DeleteDestinationInMemoryAndDbCascade()
{
  int destinationId;
  using (var context = new BreakAwayContext())
  {
    var destination = new Destination
    {
      Name = "Sample Destination",
      Lodgings = new List<Lodging>
      {
        new Lodging { Name = "Lodging One" },
        new Lodging { Name = "Lodging Two" }
      }
    };

    context.Destinations.Add(destination);
    context.SaveChanges();
    destinationId = destination.DestinationId;
  }

  using (var context = new BreakAwayContext())
  {
    var destination = context.Destinations
      .Include("Lodgings")
      .Single(d => d.DestinationId == destinationId);
```

```
    var aLodging = destination.Lodgings.FirstOrDefault();
    context.Destinations.Remove(destination);

    Console.WriteLine("State of one Lodging: {0}",
      context.Entry(aLodging).State.ToString());

    context.SaveChanges();
  }
}
```

After calling Remove on the Destination, the state of a Lodging is displayed in the console window. It is Deleted also even though we did not explicitly remove any of the Lodgings. That's because Entity Framework used client-side cascade deleting to delete the dependent Lodgings when the code explicitly deleted (Removed) the destination.

Next, when SaveChanges is called, Entity Framework sent three DELETE commands to the database, as shown in Figure 4-8. The first two are to delete the related Lodging instances that were in memory and the third to delete the Destination.

```
exec sp_executesql N'delete [dbo].[Lodgings]  where ([LodgingId] = @0)',N'@0 int',@0=1
exec sp_executesql N'delete [dbo].[Lodgings]  where ([LodgingId] = @0)',N'@0 int',@0=2
exec sp_executesql N'delete [dbo].[Destinations]  where ([DestinationId] = @0)',N'@0 int',@0=1
```

Figure 4-8. Delete commands in response to deleting a Destination and its related Lodgings

Now let's change the method. We'll remove the eager loading (Include) that pulled the Lodging data into memory along with Destination. We'll also remove all of the related code that mentions the Lodgings. Since there are no Lodgings in memory, there will be no client-side cascade delete, but the database should clean up any orphaned Lodgings because of the cascade delete defined in the database (Figure 4-7). The revised method is listed in Example 4-13.

Example 4-13. Modified DeleteDestinationInMemoryAndDbCascade code

```
private static void DeleteDestinationInMemoryAndDbCascade()
{
  int destinationId;
  using (var context = new BreakAwayContext())
  {
    var destination = new Destination
    {
      Name = "Sample Destination",
      Lodgings = new List<Lodging>
      {
        new Lodging { Name = "Lodging One" },
        new Lodging { Name = "Lodging Two" }
      }
    };

    context.Destinations.Add(destination);
    context.SaveChanges();
```

```
    destinationId = destination.DestinationId;
  }

  using (var context = new BreakAwayContext())
  {
    var destination = context.Destinations
      .Single(d => d.DestinationId == destinationId);

    context.Destinations.Remove(destination);
    context.SaveChanges();
  }

  using (var context = new BreakAwayContext())
  {
    var lodgings = context.Lodgings
      .Where(l => l.DestinationId == destinationId).ToList();

    Console.WriteLine("Lodgings: {0}", lodgings.Count);
  }
}
```

When run, the only command sent to the database is one to delete the destination. The database cascade delete will delete the related lodgings in response. When querying for the Lodgings at the end, since the database deleted the lodgings, the query will return no results and the lodgings variable will be an empty list.

Turning On or Off Client-Side Cascade Delete with Fluent Configurations

You might be working with an existing database that does not use cascade delete or you may have a policy of being explicit about data removal and not letting it happen automatically in the database. If the relationship from Lodging to Destination is optional, this is not a problem, since by convention, Code First won't use cascade delete with an optional relationship. But you may want a required relationship in your classes without leveraging cascade delete.

You may want to get an error if the user of your application tries to delete a Destination and hasn't explicitly deleted or reassigned the Lodging instances assigned to it.

For the scenarios where you want a required relationship but no cascade delete, you can explicitly override the convention and configure cascade delete behavior with the Fluent API. This is not supported with Data Annotations.

Keep in mind that if you set the model up this way, your application code will be responsible for deleting or reassigning dependent data when necessary.

The Fluent API method to use is called WillCascadeOnDelete and takes a Boolean as a parameter. This configuration is applied to a relationship, which means that you first need to specify the relationship using a Has/With pairing and then call WillCascadeOnDelete.

Working within the LodgingConfiguration class, the relationship is defined as:

```
HasRequired(l=>l.Destination)
  .WithMany(d=>d.Lodgings)
```

From there, you'll find three possible configurations to add. `WillCascadeOnDelete` is one of them, as you can see in Figure 4-9.

```
HasRequired(l=>l.Destination).WithMany(d=>d.Lodgings).|
                                            ◈ HasForeignKey<>
                                            ◈ Map
                                            ◈ WillCascadeOnDelete
```

Figure 4-9. WillCascadeOnDelete—one of the configurations you can add to a fluently described relationship

Now you can set `WillCascadeOnDelete` to `false` for this relationship:

```
HasRequired(l=>l.Destination)
  .WithMany(d=>d.Lodgings)
  .WillCascadeOnDelete(false)
```

 If you add the above code to your project, remove it again before continuing with the rest of this chapter.

This will also mean that the database schema that Code First generates will not include the cascade delete. The Delete Rule that was `Cascade` in Figure 4-7 would become `No Action`.

In the scenario where the relationship is required, you'll need to be aware of logic that will create a conflict, for example, the current required relationship between `Lodging` and `Destination` that requires that a `Lodging` instance have a `Destination` or a `DestinationId`. If you have a `Lodging` that is being change-tracked and you delete its related `Destination`, this will cause `Lodging.Destination` to become null. When `SaveChanges` is called, Entity Framework will attempt to synchronize `Lodging.DestinationId`, setting it to null. But that's not possible and an exception will be thrown with the following detailed message:

> The relationship could not be changed because one or more of the foreign-key properties is non-nullable. When a change is made to a relationship, the related foreign-key property is set to a null value. If the foreign-key does not support null values, a new relationship must be defined, the foreign-key property must be assigned another non-null value, or the unrelated object must be deleted.

The overall message here is that you have control over the cascade delete setting, but you will be responsible for avoiding or resolving possible validation conflicts caused by not having a cascade delete present.

Setting Cascade Delete Off in Scenarios That Are Not Supported by the Database

Some databases (including SQL Server) don't support multiple relationships that specify cascade delete pointing to the same table. Because Code First configures required relationships to have cascade delete, this results in an error if you have two required relationships to the same entity. You can use `WillCascadeOnDelete(false)` to turn off the cascade delete setting on one or more of the relationships. Example 4-14 shows an example of the exception message from SQL Server if you don't configure this correctly.

Example 4-14. Exception message when Code First attempts to create cascade delete where multiple relationships exist

```
System.InvalidOperationException was unhandled
  Message=The database creation succeeded, but the creation of the database objects
        did not.
  See InnerException for details.

 InnerException: System.Data.SqlClient.SqlException
   Message=Introducing FOREIGN KEY constraint 'Lodging_SecondaryContact' on table
         'Lodgings' may cause cycles or multiple cascade paths. Specify ON DELETE
         NO ACTION or ON UPDATE NO ACTION, or modify other FOREIGN KEY
         constraints. Could not create constraint. See previous errors.
```

Consider Performance Implications of Client-Side Cascade Delete

Whether you are using Code First, Database First, or Model First, you should keep in mind the performance implications of cascade delete. If you delete a principal, or "parent," without having the related object(s) in memory, the database will take care of the cascade delete. If you pull all of the related objects into memory and let the client-side cascade delete affect those related objects, then call `SaveChanges`, `SaveChanges` will send `DELETE` commands to the database for each of those related objects. There may be cases where those related objects are in memory and you do indeed want them to be deleted. But if you don't need them in memory and can rely on the database to do the cascade delete, you should consider avoiding pulling them into memory.

Exploring Many-to-Many Relationships

Entity Framework supports many-to-many relationships. Let's see how Code First responds to a many-to-many relationship between two classes when generating a database.

If you've had many-to-many relationships when using the database-first strategy, you may be familiar with the fact that Entity Framework can create many-to-many mappings when the database join table contains only the primary keys of the related entities. This mapping rule is the same for Code First.

Let's add a new `Activity` class to the model. `Activity`, shown in Example 4-15, will be related to the `Trip` class. A `Trip` can have a number of `Activities` scheduled and an Activity can be scheduled for a variety of trips. Therefore `Trip` and `Activity` will have a many-to-many relationship.

Example 4-15. A new class, Activity

```
using System.ComponentModel.DataAnnotations;
using System.Collections.Generic;

namespace Model
{
  public class Activity
  {
    public int ActivityId { get; set; }
    [Required,MaxLength(50)]
    public string Name { get; set; }

    public List<Trip> Trips { get; set; }
  }
}
```

There's a `List<Trip>` in the `Activity` class. Let's also add a `List<Activity>` to the `Trip` class for the other end of the many-to-many relationship:

```
    public List<Activity> Activities { get; set; }
```

When you run the application again, Code First will recreate the database because of the model changes. Code First convention will recognize the many-to-many relationship and build a join table in the database with the appropriate keys of the tables it's joining. The keys are both primary keys of the join table and foreign keys pointing to the joined tables, as shown in Figure 4-10.

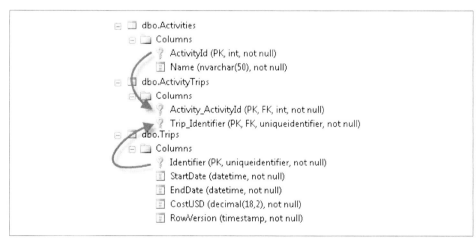

Figure 4-10. The ActivityTrips join table created by Code First for the many-to-many relationship

Notice that Code First convention created the table name by combining the names of the classes it's joining and then pluralizing the result. It also used the same pattern we've seen earlier for creating the foreign key names. In Chapter 5, which focuses on table and column mappings, you'll learn how to specify the table name and column names of the join table with configurations.

Once the many-to-many relationship exists, it behaves in just the same way that many-to-many relationships have worked in Entity Framework since the first version. You can query, add, and remove related objects by using the class properties. In the background, Entity Framework will use its knowledge of how your classes map to the database to create select, insert, update, and delete commands that incorporate the join table.

For example, the following query looks for a single trip and eager loads the related Activities:

```
var tripWithActivities = context.Trips
    .Include("Activities").FirstOrDefault();
```

The query is written against the classes with no need to be concerned about how the trip and its activities are joined in the database. Entity Framework uses its knowledge of the mappings to work out the SQL that performs the join and returns a graph that includes all of the activities that are bound to the first trip. This may not be exactly how you would construct the SQL, but remember that Entity Framework constructs the store SQL based on a pattern that can be used generically regardless of the structure of your classes or the schema of the database.

The result is a graph of the trip and its activities. Figure 4-11 shows the Trip in a debug window. You can see it has two Activities that were pulled back from the database along with the Trip.

Name	Value	Type
⊟ 🔑 tripWithActivities	{Model.Trip}	Model.Trip
⊞ 🔧 Activities	Count = 2	System.Collections.Generic.List<Model.Activity>
🔧 CostUSD	800	decimal
⊞ 🔧 EndDate	{9/14/2011 12:00:00 AM}	System.DateTime
⊞ 🔧 Identifier	{d068d5fe-55ff-4578-a312-163e07c8c7df}	System.Guid
⊞ 🔧 RowVersion	{byte[8]}	byte[]
⊞ 🔧 StartDate	{9/1/2011 12:00:00 AM}	System.DateTime

Figure 4-11. Trip and Activities graph that is a result of querying across a many-to-many relationship

Expanding the Activities in Figure 4-12 shows the details of the activities returned. Notice that there is a circular reference pointing back to the Trip that each Activity is attached to in memory.

Name	Value	Type
⊟ 🔹 tripWithActivities	{Model.Trip}	Model.Trip
⊟ 🔧 Activities	Count = 2	System.Collections.Generic.List<Model.Activity>
⊟ 🔹 [0]	{Model.Activity}	Model.Activity
🔹 ActivityId	4	int
🔹 Name	"Bicycle Touring" 🔍 ▾	string
⊞ 🔹 Trips	Count = 1	System.Collections.Generic.List<Model.Trip>
⊟ 🔹 [1]	{Model.Activity}	Model.Activity
🔹 ActivityId	5	int
🔹 Name	"Horse Riding" 🔍 ▾	string
⊞ 🔹 Trips	Count = 1	System.Collections.Generic.List<Model.Trip>
⊞ 🔹 Raw View		
🔹 CostUSD	800	decimal
⊞ 🔹 EndDate	{9/14/2011 12:00:00 AM}	System.DateTime
⊞ 🔹 Identifier	{d068d5fe-55ff-4578-a312	System.Guid
⊞ 🔹 RowVersion	{byte[8]}	byte[]
⊞ 🔹 StartDate	{9/1/2011 12:00:00 AM}	System.DateTime

Figure 4-12. Inspecting the Activities returned along with the Trip

Entity Framework took care of the joins to get across the join table without you having to be aware of its presence. In the same way, any time you do inserts, updates, or deletes within this many-to-many relationship, Entity Framework will work out the proper SQL for the join without you having to worry about it in your code.

Working with Relationships that Have Unidirectional Navigation

So far we have looked at relationships where a navigation property is defined in both classes that are involved in the relationship. However, this isn't a requirement when working with the Entity Framework.

In your domain, it may be commonplace to navigate from a Destination to its associated Lodging options, but a rarity to navigate from a Lodging to its Destination. Let's go ahead and remove the Destination property from the Lodging class (Example 4-16).

Example 4-16. Navigation property removed from Lodging class

```
public class Lodging
{
  public int LodgingId { get; set; }
  public string Name { get; set; }
  public string Owner { get; set; }
  public bool IsResort { get; set; }
  public decimal MilesFromNearestAirport { get; set; }

  public int DestinationId { get; set; }
  //public Destination Destination { get; set; }
  public List<InternetSpecial> InternetSpecials { get; set; }
```

```
  public Person PrimaryContact { get; set; }
  public Person SecondaryContact { get; set; }
}
```

Entity Framework is perfectly happy with this; it has a very clear relationship defined from Lodging to Destination with the Lodgings property in the Destination class. This still causes the model builder to look for a foreign key in the Lodging class and Lodging.DestinationId satisfies the convention.

Now let's go one step further and remove the foreign key property from the Lodging class, as shown in Example 4-17.

Example 4-17. Foreign key commented out

```
public class Lodging
{
  public int LodgingId { get; set; }
  public string Name { get; set; }
  public string Owner { get; set; }
  public bool IsResort { get; set; }
  public decimal MilesFromNearestAirport { get; set; }

  //public int DestinationId { get; set; }
  //public Destination Destination { get; set; }
}
```

 Removing DestinationId will break a previous sample, the DeleteDestinationInMemoryAndDbCascade method in Example 4-12. Comment that method out so that your solution will still compile properly.

Remember the Code First convention that will introduce a foreign key if you don't define one in your class? That same convention still works when only one navigation property is defined in the relationship. Destination still has a property that defines its relationship to Lodging. In Figure 4-13 you can see that a Destination_DestinationId column is added into the Lodgings table. You might recall that the convention for naming the foreign key column was *[Navigation Property Name]* + *[Primary Key Name]*. But we no longer have a navigation property on Lodging. If no navigation property is defined on the dependent entity, Code First will use *[Principal Type Name]* + *[Primary Key Name]*. In this case, that happens to equate to the same name.

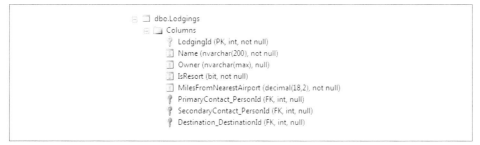

Figure 4-13. Foreign key added to the database

What if we tried to just define a foreign key and no navigation properties in either class? Entity Framework itself supports this scenario, but Code First does not. Code First requires at least one navigation property to create a relationship. If you remove both navigation properties, Code First will just treat the foreign key property as any other property in the class and will not create a foreign key constraint in the database.

Now let's change the foreign key property to something that won't get detected by convention. Let's use `LocationId` instead of `DestinationId`, as shown in Example 4-18. Remember that we have no navigation property; it's still commented out.

Example 4-18. Foreign key with unconventional name

```
public class Lodging
{
  public int LodgingId { get; set; }
  public string Name { get; set; }
  public string Owner { get; set; }
  public bool IsResort { get; set; }
  public decimal MilesFromNearestAirport { get; set; }

  public int LocationId { get; set; }
  //public Destination Destination { get; set; }
  public List<InternetSpecial> InternetSpecials { get; set; }
  public Person PrimaryContact { get; set; }
  public Person SecondaryContact { get; set; }
}
```

Thanks to `Destination.Lodgings`, Code First knows about the relationship between the two classes. But it cannot find a conventional foreign key. We've been down this road before. All we had to do was add some configuration to identify the foreign key.

In previous examples, we placed the `ForeignKey` annotation on the navigation property in the dependent class or we placed it on the foreign key property and told it which navigation property it belonged to. But we no longer have a navigation property in the dependent class. Fortunately, we can just place the data annotation on the navigation property we do have (`Destination.Lodgings`). Code First knows that `Lodging` is the dependent in the relationship, so it will search in that class for the foreign key:

```
[ForeignKey("LocationId")]
public List<Lodging> Lodgings { get; set; }
```

The Fluent API also caters to relationships that only have one navigation property. The `Has` part of the configuration must specify a navigation property, but the `With` part can be left empty if there is no inverse navigation property. Once you have specified the `Has` and `With` sections, you can call the `HasForeignKey` method you used earlier:

```
modelBuilder.Entity<Destination>()
  .HasMany(d => d.Lodgings)
  .WithRequired()
  .HasForeignKey(l => l.LocationId);
```

While a unidirectional relationship may make sense in some scenarios, we want to be able to navigate from a `Lodging` to its `Destination`. Go ahead and revert the changes to the `Lodging` class. Uncomment the `Destination` property and rename the foreign key property back to `DestinationId`, as shown in Example 4-19. You'll also need to remove the `ForeignKey` annotation from `Destination.Lodging` and remove the above Fluent API configuration if you added it.

Example 4-19. Lodging class reverted to include navigation property and conventional foreign key

```
public class Lodging
{
  public int LodgingId { get; set; }
  public string Name { get; set; }
  public string Owner { get; set; }
  public bool IsResort { get; set; }
  public decimal MilesFromNearestAirport { get; set; }

  public int DestinationId { get; set; }
  public Destination Destination { get; set; }
  public List<InternetSpecial> InternetSpecials { get; set; }
  public Person PrimaryContact { get; set; }
  public Person SecondaryContact { get; set; }
}
```

Working with One-to-One Relationships

There is one type of relationship that Code First will always require configuration for: one-to-one relationships. When you define a one-to-one relationship in your model, you use a reference navigation property in each class. If you have a reference and a collection, Code First can infer that the class with the reference is the dependent and should have the foreign key. If you have two collections, Code First knows it's many-to-many and the foreign keys go in a separate join table. However, when Code First just sees two references, it can't work out which class should have the foreign key.

Let's add a new `PersonPhoto` class to contain a photo and a caption for the people in the `Person` class. Since the photo will be for a specific person, we'll use `PersonId` as the key property. And since that is not a conventional key property, it needs to be configured as such with the `Key` Data Annotation (Example 4-20).

Example 4-20. The PersonPhoto class

```
using System.ComponentModel.DataAnnotations;
 namespace Model
{
  public class PersonPhoto
  {
    [Key]
    public int PersonId { get; set; }
    public byte[] Photo { get; set; }
    public string Caption { get; set; }

    public Person PhotoOf { get; set; }
  }
}
```

Let's also add a `Photo` property to the `Person` class, so that we can navigate both directions:

```
public PersonPhoto Photo { get; set; }
```

Remember that Code First can't determine which class is the dependent in these situations. When it attempts to build the model, an exception is thrown, telling you that it needs more information:

> Unable to determine the principal end of an association between the types 'Model.PersonPhoto' and 'Model.Person'. The principal end of this association must be explicitly configured using either the relationship fluent API or data annotations.

This problem is most easily solved by using a `ForeignKey` annotation on the dependent class to identify that it contains the foreign key. When configuring one-to-one relationships, Entity Framework requires that the primary key of the dependent also be the foreign key. In our case `PersonPhoto` is the dependent and its key, `PersonPhoto.PersonId`, should also be the foreign key. Go ahead and add in the `ForeignKey` annotation to the `PersonPhoto.PersonId` property, as shown in Example 4-21. Remember to specify the navigation property for the relationship when adding the `ForeignKey` annotation.

Example 4-21. Adding the ForeignKey annotation

```
public class PersonPhoto
{
  [Key]
  [ForeignKey("PhotoOf")]
  public int PersonId { get; set; }
  public byte[] Photo { get; set; }
  public string Caption { get; set; }
```

```
  public Person PhotoOf { get; set; }
}
```

Running the application again will successfully create the new database table, although you'll see that Entity Framework didn't deal well with pluralizing the word "Photo." We'll clean that up in Chapter 5, when you learn how to specify table names. More importantly, notice that `PersonId` is now both a PK and an FK. And if you look at the `PersonPhoto_PhotoOf` foreign key constraint details, you can see that it shows the `Peo ple.PersonId` is the primary table/column in the relationship and `PersonPhotoes.Per sonId` is the foreign key table/column (Figure 4-14). This matches our intent.

Figure 4-14. PersonPhotoes with foreign key

Earlier in this chapter, we also saw that you could place the `ForeignKey` annotation on the navigation property and specify the name of the foreign key property (in our case, that is `PersonId`). Since both classes contain a `PersonId` property, Code First still won't be able to work out which class contains the foreign key. So you can't employ the configuration in that way for this scenario.

Of course, there is also a way to configure this in the Fluent API. Let's assume for the moment that the relationship is one-to-zero-or-one, meaning a `PersonPhoto` must have a `Person` but a `Person` isn't required to have a `PersonPhoto`. We can use the `HasRe quired` and `WithOptional` combination to specify this:

```
modelBuilder.Entity<PersonPhoto>()
    .HasRequired(p => p.PhotoOf)
    .WithOptional(p => p.Photo);
```

That's actually enough for Code First to work out that `PersonPhoto` is the dependent. Based on the multiplicity we specified, it only makes sense for `Person` to be the principal and `PersonPhoto` to be the dependent, since a `Person` can exist without a `PersonPhoto` but a `PersonPhoto` must have a `Person`.

Notice that you didn't need to use `HasForeignKey` to specify that `PersonPhoto.Per sonId` is the foreign key. This is because of Entity Framework's requirement that the primary key of the dependent be used as the foreign key. Since there is no choice, Code First will just infer this for you. In fact, the Fluent API won't let you use `HasForeign Key`. In IntelliSense, the method simply isn't available after combining `HasRequired` and `WithOptional`.

Configuring One-to-One Relationships When Both Ends Are Required

Now let's tell Code First that a `Person` must have a `PersonPhoto` (i.e., it's required). With Data Annotations, you can use the same `Required` data annotation that we used earlier on `Destination.Name` and `Lodging.Name`. You can use `Required` on any type of property, not just primitive types:

```
[Required]
public PersonPhoto Photo { get; set; }
```

Now update the `Main` method to call the `InsertPerson` method you defined back in Chapter 3 and run the application again. An exception will be thrown when `Save Changes` is called. In the exception, Entity Framework's Validation API reports that the validation for the required `PersonPhoto` failed.

Ensuring that the sample code honors the required Photo

If you want to leave the `Photo` property as `Required` and avoid the validation errors, you can modify the `InsertPerson` and `UpdatePerson` methods so that they add data into the `Photo` field. For the sake of keeping the code simple, we'll just stuff a single `byte` into the `Photo`'s byte array rather than worrying about supplying an actual photo.

In the `InsertPerson` method, modify the line of code that instantiates a new `Person` object to add the `Photo` property, as shown in Example 4-22.

Example 4-22. Modifying the InsertPerson method to add a Photo to the new Person

```
var person = new Person
{
  FirstName = "Rowan",
  LastName = "Miller",
  SocialSecurityNumber = 12345678,
  Photo = new PersonPhoto { Photo = new Byte[] { 0 } }
};
```

In the `UpdatePerson` method, we'll add some code to ensure that any `Person` data you've already added before we created the `Photo` class gets a `Photo` at the same time that you update. Modify the `UpdatePerson` method as shown in Example 4-23 so that it allocates a new `PersonPhoto` when it tries to update a person without a photo.

Example 4-23. Modification to UpdatePerson to ensure existing Person data has a Photo

```
private static void UpdatePerson()
{
  using (var context = new BreakAwayContext())
  {
    var person = context.People.Include("Photo").FirstOrDefault();
    person.FirstName = "Rowena";
    if (person.Photo == null)
    {
      person.Photo = new PersonPhoto { Photo = new Byte[] { 0 } };
    }
```

```
    context.SaveChanges();
  }
}
```

The updated method will use `Include` to also retrieve the `Person`'s `Photo` when fetching the data from the database. We then check if the `Person` has a `Photo` and add a new one if they do not. Now the `Photo` requirement in the `Person` class will be fulfilled any time you execute the `InsertPerson` and `UpdatePerson` methods.

Configuring one-to-one with the Fluent API

Not surprisingly, you can also configure the same relationship with the Fluent API. But you'll need to let Code First know which class is the principal and which is the dependent. If both ends are required, this can't simply be implied from the multiplicity.

You might expect to call `HasRequired` followed by `WithRequired`. However, if you start with `HasRequired`, you will have the additional options of `WithRequiredPrincipal` and `WithRequiredDependent` in the place of `WithRequired`. These methods take into account the entity that you are configuring; that is, the entity that you selected in `model Builder.Entity` or the entity that your `EntityTypeConfiguration` class is for. Selecting `WithRequiredPrincipal` will make the entity that you are configuring the principal, meaning it contains the primary key of the relationship. Selecting `WithRequiredDepend ent` will make the entity that you are configuring the dependent, meaning it will have the foreign key of the relationship.

Assuming you are configuring `PersonPhoto`, which you want to be the dependent, you would use the following configuration:

```
modelBuilder.Entity<PersonPhoto>()
  .HasRequired(p => p.PhotoOf)
  .WithRequiredDependent(p => p.Photo);
```

Configuring a one-to-one relationship where both ends are optional works exactly the same, except you start with `HasOptional` and select either `WithOptionalPrincipal` or `WithOptionalDependent`.

Summary

In this chapter, you've seen that Code First has a lot of intelligence about relationships. Code First conventions are able to discover relationships of any multiplicity with or without a provided foreign key. But there are many scenarios where your intentions don't coincide with Code First conventions. You've learned many ways to "fix" the model by configuring with Data Annotations and the Fluent API. You should have a good understanding of how to work with relationships in the Fluent API based on its `Has`/`With` pattern.

In the next chapter, we'll look at another set of mappings in Code First that are all about how your classes map to the database, including how to map a variety of inheritance hierarchies.

CHAPTER 5

Using Conventions and Configurations for Database Mappings

So far you've learned about Code First convention and configurations that affect property attributes and those that pertain to relationships between classes. In both of these categories, Code First affected not only the model but the database as well. In this chapter, you'll learn about convention and configurations that focus on how your classes map to the database without impacting the conceptual model.

You'll start with simple mappings that allow you to specify the names of database tables, schemas and properties. You'll learn how to enable multiple classes to map to a common table, or map a single class to multiple tables. Finally, we'll walk you through a variety of inheritance scenarios.

Mapping Class Name to Database Table and Schema Name

Entity Framework uses its pluralization service (*http://msdn.microsoft.com/en-us/library/system.data.entity.design.pluralizationservices.pluralizationservice.aspx*) to infer database table names based on the class names in the model—`Destination` becomes `Destinations`, `Person` becomes `People`, etc. Your class naming conventions, however, might not be the same as your table naming conventions. You might hit a word that doesn't get pluralized properly (such as was the case with `PersonPhoto,` which became `PersonPhotoes` in Chapter 4). Or you might be mapping to an existing table with names that don't happen to align with Code First convention.

 Entity Framework's pluralization service uses pluralization for common English words. There is currently no international pluralization service.

You can use the Table Data Annotation to ensure that Code First maps your class to the correct table name. Using the Table annotation, you can also impact the name of the table's database schema.

Table naming is important to other mappings, as you'll see in this chapter, from entity splitting to inheritance hierarchies and even many-to-many mapping.

By convention, Code First will do its best to pluralize the class name and use the results as the name of the table that the class is mapped to. Additionally, all tables are assigned to the schema dbo by default.

Configuring Table and Schema Name with Data Annotations

The Table Data Annotation allows you to change the name of the table that your class maps to. In the last chapter, you may recall that Entity Framework didn't handle the PersonPhoto pluralization very well and named the table PersonPhotoes. Although the pluralization might work nicely for a class named Potato, you might want to help out with PersonPhoto:

```
[Table("PersonPhotos")]
public class PersonPhoto
```

Another example is in the original BreakAway database, which is used in both the first and second editions of *Programming Entity Framework*. The table that contains the destination information is named Locations. If you were mapping to that table, you'd want to specify the table name:

```
[Table("Locations")]
public class Destination
```

Table also has a *named parameter* for specifying the schema name. Here is how it would look together with a specified table name:

```
[Table("Locations", Schema="baga")]
public class Destination
```

Remember that for Visual Basic the syntax is a bit different for named parameters:

```
<Table("Locations", Schema:="baga")>
Public Class Destination
```

Figure 5-1 shows the Locations table with the baga schema.

The second parameter is not required, making Table("Locations") a valid annotation. However, if you want to specify the schema but not the table, you are still required to provide the first parameter. It cannot be empty, a space, or null, so you'll need to supply the name of the table.

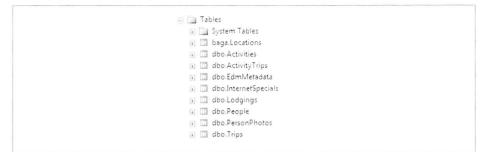

Figure 5-1. Table configuration results in baga.Locations

Configuring Table and Schema Name with the Fluent API

The Fluent API has a `ToTable` method for specifying table names and schema. It takes two parameters: the first is the table name and the second is the schema name. As with the Data Annotation, you can use the table name parameter without the schema name, but you must include the table name if you want to also specify a schema name:

```
modelBuilder.Entity<Destination>().ToTable("Locations", "baga");
```

Mapping Property Names to Database Columns

Not only can you remap the table name, but you can also alter the presumed database column name. By convention, Code First will just use the name of the property as the name of the column that it maps to, but this may not always be the case. For example, in that original BreakAway database, not only is the table name that contains destination information different than convention, but its primary field is called `LocationID`, not `DestinationId`. And the field containing the name is called `LocationName`.

Modifying the Default Column Name with Data Annotations

You may recall using the `Column` Data Annotation to modify the data type of columns earlier. The same Data Annotation is used to change the column name, as shown in Example 5-1.

Example 5-1. Specifying column names for properties using Data Annotations

```
[Column("LocationID")]
public int DestinationId { get; set; }
[Required, Column("LocationName")]
public string Name { get; set; }
```

Modifying the Default Column Name with the Fluent API

`HasColumnName` is the Fluent method used to specify a column name for a property. The column name configurations are shown in Example 5-2, as they would appear in the

DestinationConfiguration class. Notice that HasColumnName can be appended to the existing configuration for the Name property.

Example 5-2. Specifying column names for properties using the Fluent API

```
public class DestinationConfiguration :
 EntityTypeConfiguration<Destination>
{
  public DestinationConfiguration()
  {
    Property(d => d.Nam
      .IsRequired().HasColumnName("LocationName");
    Property(d => d.DestinationId).HasColumnName("LocationID");
  }
}
```

Affecting Column Names for Complex Types

In Chapter 3, you created a ComplexType from the Address class and then added an Address property to the Person class. You may recall that Code First named the columns that the Person.Address properties mapped to using the pattern Address_StreetAd dress or Address_State, etc.

You can use the same configurations to affect the column names in the Address complex type as you did for Destination previously.

Example 5-3. Configuring column names to be used in the table of any class that hosts the complex type

```
[ComplexType]
public class Address
{
  public int AddressId { get; set; }
  [MaxLength(150)]
  [Column("StreetAddress")]
  public string StreetAddress { get; set; }
  [Column("City")]
  public string City { get; set; }
  [Column("State")]
  public string State { get; set; }
  [Column("ZipCode")]
  public string ZipCode { get; set; }
}
```

Now any class that incorporates the Address complex type will use the column names specified in these Data Annotations for mapping the relevant properties.

If you configure the column names fluently, you can choose between setting the names that will be used by any class that has Address as a property or explicitly configuring each "host" class.

Examples 5-4 and 5-5 show configurations applied to the Address complex type. This will have the same effect as using the Data Annotations—all classes that host Address will use these column names.

Example 5-4. Configuring a complex type column name from the modelBuilder

```
modelBuilder.ComplexType<Address>()
  .Property(p => p.StreetAddress).HasColumnName("StreetAddress");
```

Example 5-5. Configuring the complex type column name from a configuration class

```
public class AddressConfiguration :
  ComplexTypeConfiguration<Address>
{
  public AddressConfiguration()
  {
    Property(a => a.StreetAddress).HasColumnName("StreetAddress");
  }
}
```

The effect of this configuration is that rather than let the convention create the name `Address_StreetAddress` in the Person table, the configuration will force the field name to simply be `StreetAddress`.

Example 5-6 displays examples of configuring the column name of the `StreetAddress` property by navigating through the `Person` entity. First, you'll see the configuration as it would appear in the `OnModelCreating` method and then as it would appear in a configuration class. Configuring from the `Person` class will only affect column names in the `People` table. If you have an Address property in another class, its table will not use these column names.

Example 5-6. Configuring the StreetAddress column name to be used when Address is a property of Person

```
modelBuilder.Entity<Person>()
            .Property(p => p.Address.StreetAddress)
            .HasColumnName("StreetAddress");

public class PersonConfiguration : EntityTypeConfiguration<Person>
{
  public PersonConfiguration()
  {
    Property(p => p.Address.StreetAddress)
      .HasColumnName("StreetAddress");
  }
}
```

Allowing Multiple Entities to Map to a Single Table: aka Table Splitting

Often a database table has so many columns in it that some scenarios only require you to use a subset of them, while others require access to additional column data. When mapping an entity to such a table, you may find yourself wasting resources pulling back, materializing, and carrying around unused data. *Table splitting* helps solve this problem by allowing you to break up the columns of a single table across multiple entities. Chapter 14 of the second edition of *Programming Entity Framework* covers how to map table splitting in the EDM designer. Here you'll learn how to split a table by configuring Code First.

 You may be more likely to want table splitting when mapping to an existing database where you find yourself with the scenario described above, though you might find that you want it even when letting Code First create the database for you.

Let's say that the existing database stores the photo and caption for a person in the People table rather than the separate PersonPhotos table. Since we may want access to the person's name and personal information more frequently than the photo, keeping the photo in a separate class will work out nicely. Example 5-7 provides a reminder of what the PersonPhoto class looks like, as well as the Photo property in the Person class. While we're at it, let's configure the Photo property to be an image, as we did for the Destination.Photo property in Chapter 2.

Example 5-7. The PersonPhoto class with Data Annotations

```
[Table("PersonPhotos")]
public class PersonPhoto
{
  [Key , ForeignKey("PhotoOf")]
  public int PersonId { get; set; }
  [Column(TypeName="image")]
  public byte[] Photo { get; set; }
  public string Caption { get; set; }

  public Person PhotoOf { get; set; }
}
```

By convention, Code First assumes that PersonPhoto maps to its own table, which we've configured to be named PersonPhotos.

In order to map entities into a common table, the entities must comply with the following rules:

- The entities must have a one-to-one relationship.
- The entities must share a common key.

The Person and PersonTable classes meet these requirements.

Mapping to a Common Table using Data Annotations

The Table Data Annotation is all you need to influence this mapping. Since we know that the Person entity maps to the People table, you can configure the PersonPhoto class to map to that table as well. However, you need to specify the table name for all of the involved classes. Otherwise, Entity Framework will use another convention that avoids accidental duplicate table names. You can see the result of this mistake in Figure 5-2. The PersonPhoto table is named People because of the Table configuration, so when Code First attempted to auto-name the table for the Person class and saw that People was already in use, it chose People1.

Figure 5-2. Code First convention renaming a potential duplicate table name to People1

Instead, we'll apply the table name to both classes:

```
[Table("People")]
public class Person

[Table("People")]
public class PersonPhoto
```

With this change to the model, Code First will recreate the database again. The Peo ple table now has the Photo and Caption fields (see Figure 5-3) and there is no longer a PersonPhotos table.

If you were to rerun the InsertPerson and UpdatePerson methods (recall that we modified those methods to add in single-byte photos in Chapter 4), you'll find that they continue to work without any modifications to the code. The classes are still separate. Entity Framework can work out the table mappings and perform the correct commands on the database.

What's more interesting about this mapping is that you can query one of the entities without wasting resources pulling back the table columns that are in the other entity.

If you execute a query against the Person class, for example context.People.ToList(), Entity Framework projects only those columns that map to the Person class but none of the fields that map to PersonPhoto (Example 5-8).

Figure 5-3. Photo and Caption fields in the People table

Example 5-8. SQL Query retrieving subset of table columns

```
SELECT
[Extent1].[PersonId] AS [PersonId],
[Extent1].[SocialSecurityNumber] AS [SocialSecurityNumber],
[Extent1].[FirstName] AS [FirstName],
[Extent1].[LastName] AS [LastName],
[Extent1].[Info_Weight_Reading] AS [Info_Weight_Reading],
[Extent1].[Info_Weight_Units] AS [Info_Weight_Units],
[Extent1].[Info_Height_Reading] AS [Info_Height_Reading],
[Extent1].[Info_Height_Units] AS [Info_Height_Units],
[Extent1].[Info_DietryRestrictions] AS [Info_DietryRestrictions],
[Extent1].[StreetAddress] AS [StreetAddress],
[Extent1].[City] AS [City],
[Extent1].[State] AS [State],
[Extent1].[ZipCode] AS [ZipCode]
FROM [dbo].[People] AS [Extent1]
```

Thanks to the relationship between the `Person` and `PersonPhoto` class, you can load the photo data easily, for example, eager loading with `context.People.Include("Photo")` or loading after the fact with explicit or lazy loading. This is something you can't do with scalar properties.

Lazy Loading Split Table Data

Lazy loading makes this feature shine. Although the `DbContext` we are using has lazy loading enabled by default, we have not yet discussed how to make your Code First classes leverage lazy loading. In fact, this is the same as with any simple class in Entity Framework, thanks to the POCO support introduced in Entity Framework 4 and discussed in depth in Chapter 13 of *Programming Entity Framework*. Any navigation property with the `virtual` (`Overridable` in Visual Basic) keyword applied to it will automatically be retrieved from the database when it is first accessed.

For example, you can alter the `Photo` property so that it can be lazy loaded:

```
[Required]
public virtual PersonPhoto Photo { get; set; }
```

The following example code demonstrates lazy loading the `Photo`. A query returns all of the `Person` data from the database, but the related `Photo` data is not retrieved in the query. Then the code performs some work with a particular person. In the last line, the code displays the `Caption` of the person's photo by navigating to `Person.Photo.Caption`. Since the `Photo` is not yet in memory, this call will trigger Entity Framework to run a behind-the-scenes query and retrieve that data from the database. As far as the code is concerned, the `Photo` was just there. If the `Photo` property was not virtual, or lazy loading was explicitly disabled for the context, the last line of code would throw an exception because the `Photo` property will be null:

```
var people = context.People.ToList();
var firstPerson = people[0];
SomeCustomMethodToDisplay(firstPerson.Photo.Caption);
```

 While this is a good overview, readers looking to learn more about lazy loading can find it in *Programming Entity Framework*, second edition.

Splitting a Table Using the Fluent API

Just like the Data Annotation, you need only specify the table name for the classes. And again, you must specify the table name for all of the involved classes to ensure that they all truly do map to the same table name. The following code shows the fluent configuration added directly from the `modelBuilder` instance in `OnModelCreating`. You can add them in the relevant `EntityTypeConfiguration` classes as well:

```
modelBuilder.Entity<Person>().ToTable("People");
modelBuilder.Entity<PersonPhoto>().ToTable("People");
```

Mapping a Single Entity Across Multiple Tables

Now we'll completely flip this last scenario. With the person information, it makes sense that we won't need to see a person's photo as often as we'll need to look at or work with his or her name. On the other hand, it may be more common to see the destination photo any time we retrieve a `Destination`. If you are mapping to an existing database, there's a possibility that the photo has been stored in a separate table for the sake of database normalization, performance, or some other reason. But your domain model expresses all of that data in a single class. This is when it is beneficial to map the single Destination class to grab all of the details distributed across the two database tables. This mapping is referred to as *entity splitting*.

The key to this mapping is Code First's ability to configure sets of properties to map to a particular table. It cannot be done with Data Annotations, however, because the annotations don't have the concept of a subset of properties.

The Fluent API has a Map method that lets you feed a list of properties as well as the table name. We'll use that to map some of the Destination properties to the Locations table and the others to a table named LocationPhotos. Be sure not to skip any properties!

Since there are a number of configurations on Destination at this point, the new mapping is shown along with the others inside the DestinationConfiguration class in Example 5-9.

Example 5-9. DestinationConfiguration with Entity Splitting mapping at the end

```
public class DestinationConfiguration :
  EntityTypeConfiguration<Destination>
{
  public DestinationConfiguration()
  {
    Property(d => d.Name)
     .IsRequired().HasColumnName("LocationName");
    Property(d => d.DestinationId).HasColumnName("LocationID");
    Property(d => d.Description).HasMaxLength(500);
    Property(d => d.Photo).HasColumnType("image");
    // ToTable("Locations", "baga");
    Map(m =>
        {
          m.Properties(d => new
              {d.Name, d.Country, d.Description });
          m.ToTable("Locations");
        });
    Map(m =>
        {
          m.Properties(d => new { d.Photo });
          m.ToTable("LocationPhotos");
        });
  }
}
```

The lambda expressions in the Map configuration are multiline statements, which is why you see the semicolons inside the lambda expression. Multiline lambda statements are also supported for Visual Basic (VB). The same configuration class is shown in VB in Example 5-10.

Example 5-10. DestinationConfiguration using Visual Basic syntax

```
Public Class DestinationConfiguration
  Inherits EntityTypeConfiguration(Of Destination)
  Public Sub New()
```

```
    Me.Property(Function(d) d.Name)
      .IsRequired().HasColumnName("LocationName")
    Me.Property(Function(d) d.DestinationId)
      .HasColumnName("LocationID")
    Me.Property(Function(d) d.Description).HasMaxLength(500)
    Me.Property(Function(d) d.Photo).HasColumnType("image")
    Me.Ignore(Function(d) d.TodayForecast)
    ' Me.ToTable("Locations") REM replaced by table mapping below
    Me.Map(Sub(m)
             m.Properties(Function(d) New With
               {Key d.Name, Key d.Country, Key d.Description})
               m.ToTable("Locations")
           End Sub)
    Map(Sub(m)
          m.Properties(Function(d) New With {Key d.Photo})
          m.ToTable("LocationPhotos")
        End Sub)
  End Sub
End Class
```

Notice that there are two separate Map configurations. Alternatively, you can chain one onto the end of the other, as shown in Example 5-11.

Example 5-11. Combining the mappings

```
Map(m =>
    {
      m.Properties(d => new { d.Name, d.Country, d.Description });
      m.ToTable("Locations");
    }
  .Map(m =>
      {
        m.Properties(d => new { d.Photo });
        m.ToTable("LocationPhotos");
      }
    );
```

Finally, we can see the effect on the database in Figure 5-4.

Notice that even though we mapped only the Photo property to the LocationPhotos table, Code First worked out a shared primary key and a foreign key for that table. It also created a PK/FK constraint between Locations and LocationPhotos. Interestingly, there is no cascade delete defined for the LocationPhotos table. But Entity Framework knows that if you delete a Destination, it will have to build a Delete command that spans both tables. Let's take a look at the SQL generated by Entity Framework for various CRUD operations against Destination objects.

Example 5-12 shows the code we wrote back in Chapter 2 that inserts a single Desti nation object and calls SaveChanges.

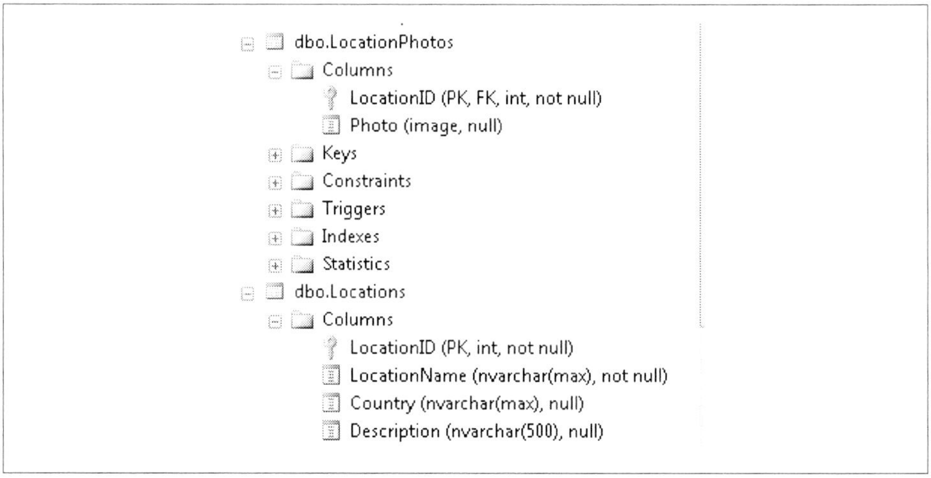

Figure 5-4. Properties from the Destination class spread across multiple tables

Example 5-12. Insert a single object that maps to two database tables

```
private static void InsertDestination()
{
  var destination = new Destination
    {
      Country = "Indonesia",
      Description = "EcoTourism at its best in exquisite Bali",
      Name = "Bali"
    };
  using (var context = new BreakAwayContext())
  {
    context.Destinations.Add(destination);
    context.SaveChanges();
  }
}
```

```
exec sp_executesql
N'insert [dbo].[Locations]([LocationName], [Country], [Description])
values (@0, @1, @2)
select [LocationID]
from [dbo].[Locations]
where @@ROWCOUNT > 0 and [LocationID] = scope_identity()',
N'@0 nvarchar(max) ,@1 nvarchar(max) ,@2 nvarchar(500)',
@0=N'Bali',@1=N'Indonesia',@2=N'EcoTourism at its best in exquisite Bali'

exec sp_executesql
N'insert [dbo].[LocationPhotos]([LocationID], [Photo])
  values (@0, null)',
N'@0 int',@0=1
```

The SQL that results first inserts data into the Locations table. In the same command, there is code to return the newly generated LocationID value. The second command then inserts a new row into LocationPhotos, including the LocationID that was returned from the first command. Since the method did not provide any photo information, the value of the Photo field inserted into that table is null.

Example 5-13 shows code to query, update, and delete Destination data. You can see by the SQL that Entity Framework handles interaction with the multiple tables as it builds commands in response to SaveChanges.

Example 5-13. Query, update and delete a Destination

```
using (var context = new BreakAwayContext())
{
  var destinations = context.Destinations.ToList();
  var destination = destinations[0];
  destination.Description += "Trust us, you'll love it!";
  context.SaveChanges();
  context.Destinations.Remove(destination);
  context.SaveChanges();
}
```

```
--RESPONSE TO QUERY
SELECT
[Extent1].[LocationID] AS [LocationID],
[Extent2].[LocationName] AS [LocationName],
[Extent2].[Country] AS [Country],
[Extent2].[Description] AS [Description],
[Extent1].[Photo] AS [Photo]
FROM  [dbo].[LocationPhotos] AS [Extent1]
INNER JOIN [dbo].[Locations] AS [Extent2] ON [Extent1].[LocationID] = [Extent2].
[LocationID]

-RESPONSE TO UPDATE
exec sp_executesql
N'update [dbo].[Locations]
  set [Description] = @0
  where ([LocationID] = @1)',
N'@0 nvarchar(500),@1 int',
@0='Trust us, you''ll love it!',@1=1

--RESPONSE TO DELETE
exec sp_executesql N'delete [dbo].[LocationPhotos]
where ([LocationID] = @0)',N'@0 int',@0=1

exec sp_executesql N'delete [dbo].[Locations]
where ([LocationID] = @0)',N'@0 int',@0=1
```

Now that we've taken a look at entity splitting, let's put all the Destination data back into a single table. If you've been following along in Visual Studio, remove the entity splitting configuration we just added and reinstate the single ToTable call to map Destination to the Locations table:

```
ToTable("Locations", "baga");
```

Controlling Which Types Get Mapped to the Database

Each time you've added a class to the model, you've also had to add a DbSet into the BreakAwayContext. The DbSet serves two functions. The first is that it returns a queryable set of a particular type. The second is that it lets DbModelBuilder know that the type referred to in each set should be included in the model.

But this is not the only way to ensure that a type becomes part of your model. There are three ways for a type to be included in the model:

1. Expose a DbSet of the type in the context.
2. Have a reference to the type in another type that is mapped (i.e., the type is reachable from another type in the model).
3. Reference a type from any Fluent API call on the DbModelBuilder.

You've seen the first in action. Let's check out the other two.

We'll add a new class to the model: Reservation.

Example 5-14. The new Reservation class

```
namespace Model
{
  public class Reservation
  {
    public int ReservationId { get; set; }
    public DateTime DateTimeMade { get; set; }
    public Person Traveler { get; set; }
    public Trip Trip { get; set; }
    public DateTime PaidInFull { get; set; }
  }
}
```

If you run the application, the DbModelBuilder will not be aware of this type. There's no DbSet<Reservation> and neither of the other two conditions listed above have been met. Therefore, the model will not change and the database will not get recreated. If you look at the database, there is no Reservations table.

Now, let's go to the Person class and add a property so that we can see all of the Reservations made by a Person:

```
    public List<Reservation> Reservations { get; set; }
```

Run the app again, and now you'll see a Reservations table in the database. You can see the new table in Figure 5-5.

Figure 5-5. New Reservations table

By convention, because `Person` is in the model and `Person` is aware of the `Reservation` class, Code First pulls `Reservation` into the model as well.

Now let's look at the third convention for including a class in the model—providing a configuration.

First, comment out the `Reservations` property in `Person` to be sure you're back to the state where the `Reservation` class will not be discovered by the model:

```
// public List<Reservation> Reservations { get; set; }
```

Add a fluent configuration for reservation. The effect will be the same whether you encapsulate the configuration into an `EntityTypeConfiguration` class and add it into the `modelBuilder.Configurations` or if you just call `modelBuilder.Entity` for the type directly in `OnModelCreating`. Just to keep things organized, we'll create a separate configuration class, shown in Example 5-15.

Example 5-15. An empty configuration class for Reservation

```
public class ReservationConfiguration :
  EntityTypeConfiguration<Reservation>
{
}
```

Notice that we've done nothing more than declare the class. There's no code in it. This is enough to allow you to add the class to the `DbModelBuilder` configurations, which will ensure that `Reservation` is included in the model and maps to the database table, `Reservations`:

```
modelBuilder.Configurations.Add(new ReservationConfiguration());
```

Now that you've seen the conventional behavior that causes Code First to include a class in its model, let's look at how to configure the model to exclude a class.

Preventing Types from Being Included in the Model

You may have classes defined in your application that exist for purposes that do not require them to be persisted in the database. And even if you do not define a `DbSet` or any configurations for them, it's possible that they are reachable by another type and therefore pulled into the model—creating an expectation that the class will be involved in queries or updates to the database.

However, you can explicitly tell Code First to ignore a class that should not be part of the model.

Using Data Annotations to ignore types

The `NotMapped` annotation can be applied to a class to instruct Code First to exclude the type from the model:

```
[NotMapped]
public class MyInMemoryOnlyClass
```

Using Fluent Configuration to ignore types

With the Fluent API, you'll use the `Ignore` method to prevent types from being pulled into the model. If you want to ignore a class, you need to do this directly from the `DbModelBuilder`, not inside of an `EntityTypeConfiguration`:

```
modelBuilder.Ignore<MyInMemoryOnlyClass>();
```

Understanding Property Mapping and Accessibility

There are a variety of factors that affect whether or not properties in your classes are recognized and mapped by Code First. Following is a list of rules to be aware of when defining properties in your classes, what to expect from convention, and how to change the default mapping with configuration.

Scalar Property Mapping

Scalar properties are only mapped if they can be converted to a type that is supported by EDM.

The valid EDM types are `Binary`, `Boolean`, `Byte`, `DateTime`, `DateTimeOffset`, `Decimal`, `Double`, `Guid`, `Int16`, `Int32`, `Int64`, `SByte`, `Single`, `String`, `Time`.

Scalar properties that can't be mapped to an EDM type are ignored (e.g., enums and unsigned integers).

Accessibility of Properties, Getters, and Setters

1. A public property will be automatically mapped by Code First.
2. The setter can be marked with a more restrictive accessor, but the getter must remain public for the property to be mapped automatically.
3. A nonpublic property must be configured using the Fluent API in order to be mapped by Code First.

In the case of nonpublic properties, this means you need to be able to access the property from wherever you perform the configuration.

For example, if you had a Person class with an internal Name property that lived in the same assembly as your PersonContext class, you could call modelBuilder.Entity<Person>().Property(p => p.Name) in the OnModelCreating method of your Person context. This would cause the property to be included in your model.

However, if Person and PersonContext were defined in separate assemblies, you could add a PersonConfiguration class (EntityConfiguration<Person>) to the same assembly as the Person class and perform the configuration inside the configuration class. This would require that the assembly containing the domain classes have a reference to *EntityFramework.dll*. The PersonConfig configuration class could then be registered in the OnModelCreating method of the PersonContext.

A similar approach can be used for protected and private properties. However, the configuration class must be nested inside the class that is part of the model, so that it can access private and protected properties. Here is an example of such a class, which hides the Name with a private modifier but allows external code to set Name using a CreatePerson method. The nested PersonConfig class has access to the locally scoped Name property:

```
public class Person
{
  public int PersonId { get; set; }
  private string Name { get; set; }

  public class PersonConfig : EntityTypeConfiguration<Person>
  {
    public PersonConfig()
    {
      Property(b => b.Name);
    }
  }

  public string GetName()
  {
    return this.Name;
  }

  public static Person CreatePerson(string name)
  {
    return new Person { Name = name };
  }
}
```

When the configuration class is nested, you can register it like this:

```
modelBuilder.Configurations.Add(new Person.PersonConfig());
```

A common scenario people ask about is preventing developers from modifying a particular property (e.g., PersonId) in code by setting its setter to private or internal. This is possible thanks to the second rule listed above: the setter can be marked with a more restrictive accessor, but the getter must remain public for the property to be mapped automatically. Entity Framework will use reflection to access a nonpublic setter, but *this is not supported when running in medium trust.* With the exception of medium trust scenarios, this means that the context will be able to populate restricted properties when materializing objects as a result of a query or an insert. The context will still be able to set the value of that property as a result of queries or inserts—even if the context and domain class are in separate assemblies or namespaces. This will work with key values as well as nonkey values.

Preventing Properties from Being Included in the Model

By convention, all public properties that have both a getter and a setter will be included in the model.

Code First uses the same configuration methods—`NotMapped` in Data Annotations and `Ignore` in Fluent configurations—to exclude properties from classes.

A typical example of a property that you might not want to store in the database is one that performs a calculation using other properties in a class. For example, you might want to have easy access to a person's full name based on their first and last name. The class can calculate that on the fly and you may have no need to store it in the database.

If a property has only a getter or a setter, but not both, it will not be included in the model.

If you had the following property, `FullName`, in the `Person` class, it would not get mapped because it has a getter but no setter:

```
public string FullName
{
    get { return String.Format("{0} {1}",
                        FirstName.Trim(), LastName); }
}
```

However, you might have a property with both a getter and a setter that you don't want persisted in the database. For example, the `Destination` class might have a string with the current forecast in it. But you don't want to discover the forecast on-demand, and you might have a routine elsewhere in the application that populates the forecast:

```
private string _todayForecast;

public string TodayForecast
{
    get { return _todayForecast; }
    set { _todayForecast = value; }
}
```

That's a case where you won't want to persist the forecast info in the database. Entity Framework should not include the property when querying or modifying the database table that maps to `Destination`.

Data Annotations for Ignoring a Property

With Data Annotations, you can apply the `NotMapped` attribute:

```
[NotMapped]
public string TodayForecast
```

Fluent Configuration for Ignoring a Property

In the Fluent API, you can configure the entity to ignore a property. Here's an example of using the `Ignore` method in the `DestinationConfiguration` class:

```
Ignore(d => d.TodayForecast);
```

Note that there is a known bug when using `NotMapped` or `Ignore` on private properties. You can see a description of the problem in an MSDN Connect item (*http://connect.microsoft.com/VisualStudio/feedback/details/675167/ef-cf-notmappedattribute-ignored-on-private-properties*). An August 18, 2011, comment by Microsoft in the same issue says, "This has been fixed and will be released in the next major release of Code First."

Mapping Inheritance Hierarchies

Entity Framework supports a variety of inheritance hierarchies in the model. Whether you define your model with Code First, Model First, or Database First has no bearing on the types of inheritance or how Entity Framework works with these types for querying, change tracking, and updating data.

Chapter 14 of *Programming Entity Framework* addresses inheritance in detail. In the following sections, we'll focus on how to achieve the desired inheritance in your model, but we won't spend a lot of time on interacting with the types in the hierarchy.

Working with Code First's Default Inheritance: Table Per Hierarchy (TPH)

Table Per Hierarchy (TPH) describes mapping inherited types to a single database table that uses a discriminator column to differentiate one subtype from another. When you create inheritance in your model, this is how Code First convention will infer the table mapping by default. To see this in action, let's make two changes to the model. First, we'll remove the IsResort property from Lodging and then create a separate Resort class that inherits from Lodging. Example 5-16 displays these classes.

Example 5-16. Modified Lodging class and a new Resort class that derives from Lodging

```
public class Lodging
{
  public int LodgingId { get; set; }

  [Required]
  [MaxLength(200)]
  [MinLength(10)]
  public string Name { get; set; }
  public string Owner { get; set; }
  // public bool IsResort { get; set; }
  public decimal MilesFromNearestAirport { get; set; }
  [InverseProperty("PrimaryContactFor")]
  public Person PrimaryContact { get; set; }
  [InverseProperty("SecondaryContactFor")]
  public Person SecondaryContact { get; set; }
  public int DestinationId { get; set; }
  public Destination Destination { get; set; }
  public List<InternetSpecial> InternetSpecials { get; set; }
}

public class Resort : Lodging
{
  public string Entertainment { get; set; }
  public string Activities { get; set; }
}
```

Figure 5-6 shows the impact on the database using Code First convention.

```
dbo.Lodgings
  Columns
    LodgingId (PK, int, not null)
    Name (nvarchar(200), not null)
    Owner (nvarchar(max), null)
    MilesFromNearestAirport (decimal(18,2), not null)
    DestinationId (FK, int, not null)
    Entertainment (nvarchar(max), null)
    Activities (nvarchar(max), null)
    Discriminator (nvarchar(128), not null)
    PrimaryContact_PersonId (FK, int, null)
    SecondaryContact_PersonId (FK, int, null)
```

Figure 5-6. Discriminator and Resort type fields in Lodgings table

The Resort information is stored in the Lodgings table, and Code First created a column called Discriminator. Notice that it is non-nullable and its type is nvarchar(128). By default, Code First will use the type name of each type in the hierarchy as the value

stored in the discriminator column. For example, if you add and run the InsertLodg
ing method (Example 5-17), the INSERT command generated by Entity Framework puts
the string "Lodging" into the Discriminator column in the new database row.

Example 5-17. Code to insert a new Lodging type

```
private static void InsertLodging()
{
  var lodging = new Lodging
  {
    Name = "Rainy Day Motel",
    Destination=new Destination
    {
      Name="Seattle, Washington",
      Country="USA"
    }
  };

  using (var context = new BreakAwayContext())
  {
    context.Lodgings.Add(lodging);
    context.SaveChanges();
  }
}
```

Alternatively, Example 5-18 shows code that specifically instantiates a new Resort type.

Example 5-18. Code to insert a new Resort type

```
private static void InsertResort()
{
  var resort = new Resort {
    Name = "Top Notch Resort and Spa",
    MilesFromNearestAirport=30,
    Activities="Spa, Hiking, Skiing, Ballooning",
    Destination=new Destination{
                Name="Stowe, Vermont",
                Country="USA"}
  };
  using (var context = new BreakAwayContext())
  {
    context.Lodgings.Add(resort);
    context.SaveChanges();
  }
}
```

This time, Entity Framework will insert the string "Resort" into the Discriminator column in the database.

This conventional behavior is based on the possibility that you might add more derived
Lodging types. If the discriminator column was simply a Boolean that indicated if the
Lodging was a Resort or not, there would be no room to expand the hierarchy. This
flexibility works well for conventional behavior.

Customizing the TPH Discriminator Field with the Fluent API

You do have the ability to specifically configure the name and type of the discriminator column as well as the possible values used for delineating the various types. You can do this with the Fluent API.

 There is no Data Annotation to customize the TPH mapping.

You employ the same `Map` configuration that you used for the entity splitting above. That allows you to include a few configurations at once.

 Some configurations are only available inside of the `Map` method.

Example 5-19 shows a configuration added to the `LodgingConfiguration` class.

Example 5-19. Configuring the discriminator column name and possible values

```
Map(m =>
    {
        m.ToTable("Lodgings");
        m.Requires("LodgingType").HasValue("Standard");
    })
.Map<Resort>(m =>
    {
        m.Requires("LodgingType").HasValue("Resort");
    });
```

Notice we're seeing some new configuration methods—`Requires` and `HasValue`. `Requires` is a configuration that is specifically there to define a discriminator column. `HasValue` is also specific to configuring discriminators. You can use `HasValue` to specify what value is used for a particular type. We'll tell Code First to use `LodgingType` as the name of the discriminator column rather than use the conventional name, `Discrimina tor`. By convention, Code First uses the class name as the discriminator value (for example, "Lodging"). Instead we'll tell it to use "`Standard`" for the `Lodging` base class. Once you begin specifying discriminator values, you need to configure all of them, even if, like "Resort", they match convention.

You might know that the only derived type you'll ever have for `Lodging` is `Resort` and therefore decide that a `Boolean`, such as `IsResort`, will suffice. In that case, the value will be a `Boolean`. You don't need to tell Code First that it is a `Boolean`. Just supply the desired values and Code First will type the discriminator column accordingly.

The mapping to turn the discriminator into a `Boolean` field called `IsResort` is shown in Example 5-20.

Example 5-20. Configuring a discriminator column to be a boolean

```
Map(m =>
{
  m.ToTable("Lodging");
  m.Requires("IsResort").HasValue(false);
})
.Map<Resort>(m =>
{
  m.Requires("IsResort").HasValue(true);
});
```

The resulting `bit` column, `IsResort`, is shown in Figure 5-7.

Figure 5-7. The renamed discriminator column, IsResort

Configuring Table Per Type (TPT) Hierarchy

While TPH contains all of the types for a hierarchy in a single table, Table Per Type (TPT) only stores properties from the base class in a single table. Additional properties defined on a derived type are stored in a separate table with a foreign key back to the core table. If your database schema uses separate tables for a hierarchy, you'll need to explicitly configure the derived types to follow suit. This is a simple configuration where all you need to do is specify the table name of a derived type. You can do that with Data Annotations or the Fluent API.

Here's the configured `Resort` type:

```
[Table("Resorts")]
public class Resort : Lodging
{
  public string Entertainment { get; set; }
  public string Activities { get; set; }
}
```

The combination of the inheritance and the Table Data Annotation will tell Code First to create a new table for the Resort type, and because it inherits from Lodging, it will inherit the Lodging's key property.

TPT or TPH? How to Choose?

Alex James from the Entity Framework team has a blog post called "Tip 12—How to choose an Inheritance Strategy" (*http://blogs.msdn.com/b/alexj/archive/2009/04/15/tip -12-choosing-an-inheritance-strategy.aspx*) that you might want to check out if you would like some additional guidance on choosing an inheritance strategy.

Figure 5-8 shows the Lodgings and new Resorts table in the database. Notice that Lodgings no longer has a discriminator or the Resort fields (Entertainment and Activities).

```
⊟ ▦ dbo.Lodgings
  ⊟ ▭ Columns
      ⚷ LodgingId (PK, int, not null)
      ▦ Name (nvarchar(200), not null)
      ▦ Owner (nvarchar(max), null)
      ▦ MilesFromNearestAirport (decimal(18,2), not null)
      ⚷ DestinationId (FK, int, not null)
      ⚷ PrimaryContact_PersonId (FK, int, null)
      ⚷ SecondaryContact_PersonId (FK, int, null)
⊟ ▦ dbo.Resorts
  ⊟ ▭ Columns
      ⚷ LodgingId (PK, FK, int, not null)
      ▦ Entertainment (nvarchar(max), null)
      ▦ Activities (nvarchar(max), null)
  ⊟ ▭ Keys
      ⚷ PK_Resorts__D4C8F72B1A14E395
      ⚷ Resort_TypeConstraint_From_Lodging_To_Resorts
```

Figure 5-8. TPT configuration resulting in a Resorts table

The new Resorts table has a LodgingId column that is a primary key and a foreign key, the latter of which is named for clarity: Resort_TypeConstraint_From_Lodg ing_To_Resorts.

For the curious, there is no cascade delete defined on the Resort_Type Constraint_From_Lodging_To_Resorts key. Entity Framework will take care of deleting data from both tables when required.

When you add a new Resort and SaveChanges, this triggers Entity Framework to first add a new row in the Lodging table with the appropriate values, return the new

---

LodgingId value, and then insert a new row into `Resorts` including the `LodgingId` value that came from the new row in the `Lodgings` table.

With the Fluent API you can use the `ToTable` mappings to achieve the TPT mapping as well. Again, you need only specify the table name for the derived entity, `Resort`, so that Code First will create the extra table and constraint that you saw in Figure 5-8. Example 5-21 shows that mapping when it's built directly from the `modelBuilder` instance.

Example 5-21. In-line ToTable mapping used for TPT inheritance

```
modelBuilder.Entity<Resort>().ToTable("Resorts");
```

You could also start with the base class configuration and use the `Map` method to get to the Resort type (Example 5-22).

Example 5-22. Mapping ToTable within the Map method

```
modelBuilder.Entity<Lodging>()
    .Map<Resort>(m =>
    {
      m.ToTable("Resorts");
    }
  );
```

If you want to be explicit, you can specify the table name for each of the types in the hierarchy. In this case, the `Lodgings` table is already presumed by convention, but with a more detailed configuration, the intent is more clear to someone reading the code as shown in Example 5-23.

Example 5-23. Mapping ToTable for a TPT inheritance from base entity

```
modelBuilder.Entity<Lodging>().Map(m =>
    {
      m.ToTable("Lodgings");
    }).Map<Resort>(m =>
    {
      m.ToTable("Resorts");
    });
```

What's interesting about this last variation is that you can map a derived class from its base class configuration. You would not be able to start with `Entity<Resort>` and then add `Map<Lodging>` to it.

All three variations of building this mapping achieve the same end. But now you have some options that you might want to choose from to better align with your coding style.

Configuring for Table Per Concrete Type (TPC) Inheritance

Table Per Concrete Type (TPC) is similar to TPT, except that all the properties for each type are stored in separate tables. There is no core table that contains data common to all types in the hierarchy. This allows you to map an inheritance hierarchy to tables with overlapping (common) fields. This can be useful when you set ancient data aside in a spare table. Perhaps we're mapping Lodgings and Resorts to a table where the resort table also contains Name, Owner, and MilesFromNearestAirport. You can configure your hierarchy to map to tables with this schema using the Fluent API.

 There is no Data Annotation support for this mapping.

Let's change the mapping for the Lodging/Resort hierarchy once again.

TPC mapping is configured using the MapInheritedProperties method, which is only accessible from within the Map method. And since we also need a separate table for the derived class (that will be duplicating the inherited properties), we can combine the Table configuration and the MapInheritedProperties configuration.

Note that you must include the ToTable mapping for the base entity this time. With the TPT mapping this wasn't required, but with TPC, it is:

```
modelBuilder.Entity<Lodging>()
 .Map(m =>
 {
   m.ToTable("Lodgings");
 })
 .Map<Resort>(m =>
 {
   m.ToTable("Resorts");
   m.MapInheritedProperties();
 });
```

MapInheritedProperties is essentially telling Code First that it should remap all the properties that are inherited from the base class to new columns in the table for the derived type.

 If you are following along in Visual Studio, you should wait until reading the next section before running this code.

Avoiding Mapping Exceptions with TPC

If you attempt to run the existing application to check out this configuration, you will get an exception that details a mapping conflict as the DbModelBuilder attempts to create the new model. This is thanks to a conflict with the Lodging class.

TPC requires that relationships in any of the classes in the TPC hierarchy be expressed with an explicit foreign key property. Take a look at the Lodging class, which is listed as a reminder in Example 5-24.

Example 5-24. A reminder of the Lodging class

```
public class Lodging
{
  public int LodgingId { get; set; }

  public string Name { get; set; }
  public string Owner { get; set; }
  public decimal MilesFromNearestAirport { get; set; }
  public List<InternetSpecial> InternetSpecials { get; set; }

  public Person PrimaryContact { get; set; }
  public Person SecondaryContact { get; set; }
  public int DestinationId { get; set; }
  public Destination Destination { get; set; }
}
```

While the navigation to `Destination` is complemented by the `DestinationId` property, there are two navigation reference properties that do not have a foreign key property: `PrimaryContact` and `SecondaryContact`. Code First leverages the database foreign key fields to take care of persisting the relationship. If you've been using Entity Framework since the first version, you may recognize this as *independent associations*, which were the only option for building relationships in Visual Studio 2008. Foreign Key associations, where we can have a foreign key property such as `DestinationId` in the class, were introduced to Entity Framework in Visual Studio 2010 and .NET 4. TPC can't work with classes that have independent associations in them.

To fix this problem, you'll have to add foreign key properties into the `Lodging` class. To some developers, this is a painful pill to swallow—being forced to have your domain classes comply with Entity Framework's rules in order to participate. But unfortunately, as you may have gathered by this point, many mappings in Code First are simpler to achieve when there's a foreign key property available.

Remember that in our domain, it's possible that a `Lodging` has neither a `PrimaryContact` nor a `SecondaryContact`. When we added the `PrimaryContact` and `SecondaryContact` navigation properties in Chapter 4, Code First convention inferred them to be nullable (aka `Optional`). The new foreign key properties will be integers, which are by default non-nullable. You'll run into a conflict because it won't be possible to have an optional contact if you are required to have a value in its foreign key. Therefore, we'll make the new foreign key properties nullable as well. Notice the use of the `Nullable<T>` generic when declaring the new properties, `PrimaryContactId` and `SecondaryContactId`, in Example 5-25.

Example 5-25. Lodging class with nullable foreign keys

```
abstract public class Lodging
{
  public int LodgingId { get; set; }

  public string Name { get; set; }
  public string Owner { get; set; }
```

```
    public decimal MilesFromNearestAirport { get; set; }

    public List<InternetSpecial> InternetSpecials { get; set; }
    public Nullable<int> PrimaryContactId { get; set; }
    public Person PrimaryContact { get; set; }
    public Nullable<int> SecondaryContactId { get; set; }
    public Person SecondaryContact { get; set; }
    public int DestinationId { get; set; }
    public Destination Destination { get; set; }
}
```

We're not quite done yet. If you recall from Chapter 4, Code First will not be able to recognize unconventional foreign key properties without some help. These new properties do not match any of the three possible patterns that Code First will use to detect foreign keys (e.g., `PersonId`). So you'll need to use the `HasForeignKey` mapping you learned about in Example 4-3.

Example 5-26 shows the two existing configurations for these properties that are in the `LodgingConfiguration` class. We've modified them by adding the `HasForeignKey` mapping to each one.

Example 5-26. Fixing up the model for unconventional foreign key properties

```
HasOptional(l => l.PrimaryContact)
  .WithMany(p => p.PrimaryContactFor)
  .HasForeignKey(p=>p.PrimaryContactId);

HasOptional(l => l.SecondaryContact)
  .WithMany(p => p.SecondaryContactFor)
  .HasForeignKey(p => p.SecondaryContactId);
```

Finally all of the pieces are in place for the TPC inheritance. The model will validate and, as you can see in Figure 5-9, indeed, all of the inherited fields from the `Lodging` class are now in the `Resorts` table. And thanks to all of the work we did to help Code First work out the foreign keys, those are properly configured in the `Resorts` table as well.

Equally important is that the console application methods we wrote to insert `Lodg` `ings` and to insert `Resorts` succeed at their tasks.

 When working with an EDMX file, it is possible to specify which properties to overlap in a TPC hierarchy. With Code First, you can't filter out which properties to overlap. `MapInheritedProperties` will always cause all of the properties to be mapped to the derived table(s).

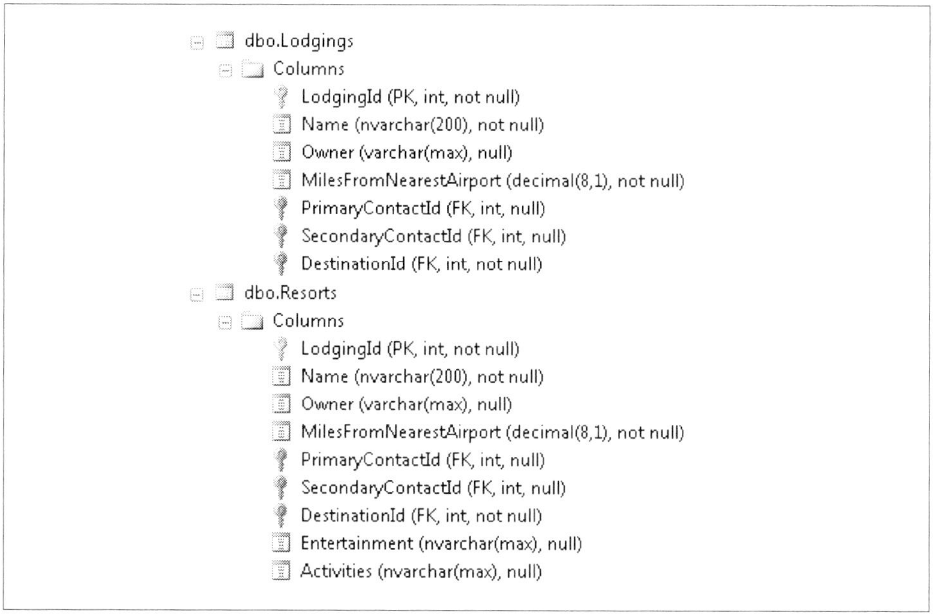

Figure 5-9. Resorts table designed for a TPC hierarchy mapping

Working with Abstract Base Classes

All of the inheritance types you've seen work whether your base class is one that you can instantiate or if it's abstract. But we think it will be helpful to take a quick look at using abstract base classes when modeling with Code First.

Let's modify the Lodging to be an abstract base class. That means we'll never use Lodging directly. It can't be instantiated. Instead, we will only ever work with classes that derive from it. In Example 5-27, we'll add a second derived class: Hostel.

Example 5-27 lists all three classes.

Example 5-27. The abstract base class, Lodging, with its derived classes, Resort and Hostel

```
abstract public class Lodging
{
  public int LodgingId { get; set; }
  public string Name { get; set; }
  public string Owner { get; set; }
  public decimal MilesFromNearestAirport { get; set; }

  public List<InternetSpecial> InternetSpecials { get; set; }
  public Nullable<int> PrimaryContactId { get; set; }
  public Person PrimaryContact { get; set; }
  public Nullable<int> SecondaryContactId { get; set; }
  public Person SecondaryContact { get; set; }
  public int DestinationId { get; set; }
  public Destination Destination { get; set; }
```

```
}

public class Resort : Lodging
{
  public string Entertainment { get; set; }
  public string Activities { get; set; }
}

public class Hostel: Lodging
{
  public int MaxPersonsPerRoom { get; set; }
  public bool PrivateRoomsAvailable { get; set; }
}
```

 When you change Lodging to be an abstract class, this means you can no longer instantiate Lodging directly. Any code that you may have in the console app that does instantiate Lodging will cause compilation errors, so you should remove or comment out any methods that contain such code. A great trick is to surround the method with the #if/ #endif processor directive and use false for the if logic. For example:

```
#if false
private static void InsertLodging()
  {
    var lodging = new Lodging
    {
      Name = "Rainy Day Motel",
      Destination = new Destination
      {
        Name = "Seattle, Washington",
        Country = "USA"
      }
    };

    using (var context = new BreakAwayContext())
    {
      context.Lodgings.Add(lodging);
      context.SaveChanges();
    }
  }
#endif
```

To include the code again, change the directive to #if true.

We've removed the TPC configuration so the resulting model and database table is purely based on Code First convention, which means that the inheritance will revert to TPH. All of the fields from the derived classes are contained in the Lodgings table. You can see in Figure 5-10 that even though Lodging is an abstract class, the effect on the database is no different than it was with the default TPH mapping when Lodging was not abstract. However, since we have another derived class, there are new properties included for the Hostel type.

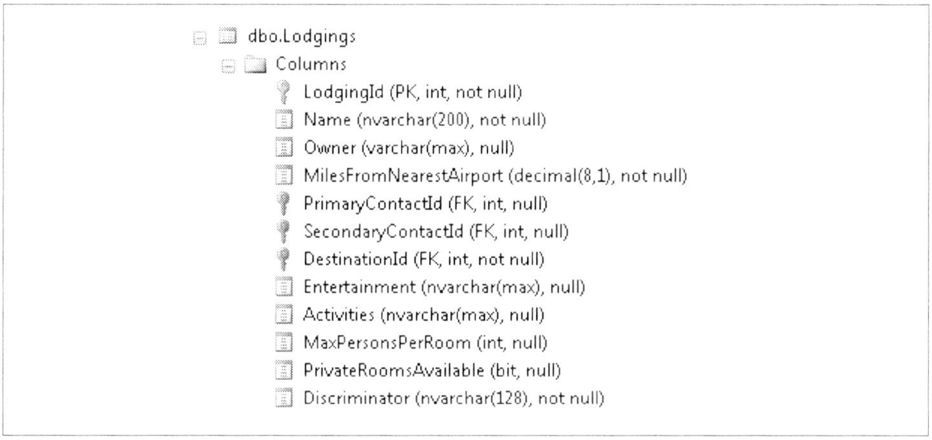

Figure 5-10. Default TPH setup with an abstract base class

Example 5-28 shows a series of methods to insert a new Resort and a new Hostel, and then query all Lodgings to see what we've got in the database.

Example 5-28. Code to insert a Resort, then insert a Hostel, and finally to query Lodgings

```
private static void InsertResort()
{
  var resort = new Resort
  {
    Name = "Top Notch Resort and Spa",
    MilesFromNearestAirport = 30,
    Activities = "Spa, Hiking, Skiing, Ballooning",
    Destination = new Destination { Name = "Stowe, Vermont",
                                    Country = "USA" }
                                  };
  using (var context = new BreakAwayContext())
  {
    context.Lodgings.Add(resort);
    context.SaveChanges();
  }
}

private static void InsertHostel()
{
  var hostel = new Hostel
  {
    Name = "AAA Budget Youth Hostel",
    MilesFromNearestAirport = 25,
    PrivateRoomsAvailable=false,
    Destination = new Destination {
                    Name = "Hanksville, Vermont",
                    Country = "USA" }
                  };
  using (var context = new BreakAwayContext())
  {
```

```
    context.Lodgings.Add(hostel);
    context.SaveChanges();
  }
}

private static void GetAllLodgings()
{
  var context = new BreakAwayContext();
  var lodgings = context.Lodgings.ToList();
  foreach (var lodging in lodgings)
  {
    Console.WriteLine("Name: {0}  Type: {1}",
      lodging.Name, lodging.GetType().ToString());
  }
  Console.ReadKey();
}
```

When Entity Framework sends the INSERT commands to the database, it populates the Discriminator column with "Resort" for the Resort class and "Hostel" for the Hostel type. When retrieving all Lodgings, it filters on Resort and Hostel discriminators, as shown in the SQL listed in Example 5-29.

Example 5-29. SQL to retrieve all of the known types that derive from Lodging

```
SELECT
[Extent1].[Discriminator] AS [Discriminator],
[Extent1].[LodgingId] AS [LodgingId],
[Extent1].[Name] AS [Name],
[Extent1].[Owner] AS [Owner],
[Extent1].[MilesFromNearestAirport] AS [MilesFromNearestAirport],
[Extent1].[PrimaryContactId] AS [PrimaryContactId],
[Extent1].[SecondaryContactId] AS [SecondaryContactId],
[Extent1].[DestinationId] AS [DestinationId],
[Extent1].[Entertainment] AS [Entertainment],
[Extent1].[Activities] AS [Activities],
[Extent1].[MaxPersonsPerRoom] AS [MaxPersonsPerRoom],
[Extent1].[PrivateRoomsAvailable] AS [PrivateRoomsAvailable]
FROM [dbo].[Lodgings] AS [Extent1]
WHERE [Extent1].[Discriminator] IN ('Resort','Hostel')
```

Why does it use the discriminators instead of simply returning all of the lodging data? This is to cover the scenario in which there are other types in the database that aren't part of the model.

Figure 5-11 shows the output into the console after the items inserted in the first two methods are retrieved in the GetAllLodgings method.

You can modify the mappings to turn this hierarchy into a TPT or TPC mapping with Code First. For example, if you specify table names for both the Resort and Hostel class while the Lodging class is abstract, you'll end up with three database tables: Resorts, Hostels, and Lodgings. The code in Example 5-28 will work with no changes. SQL commands will span and join the tables as necessary, just as they did when Lodging was not abstract. All of the behavior around abstract base classes in the model when you're

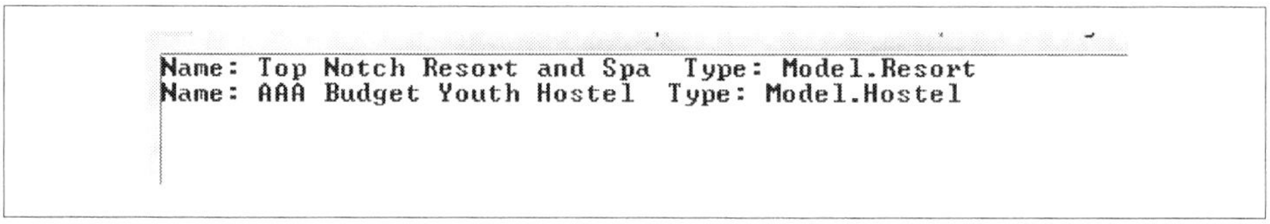

```
Name: Top Notch Resort and Spa   Type: Model.Resort
Name: AAA Budget Youth Hostel   Type: Model.Hostel
```

Figure 5-11. Output to console window

using Code First simply follows EF's behavior with abstract base classes since the first version of Entity Framework. The only difference is that you are defining the model in a new way.

Now that we've explored abstract base classes, go ahead and remove the abstract keyword from Lodging so that we can create instances of it again. You can also re-enable any of the methods you commented out when we made Lodging abstract:

```
public class Lodging
```

Mapping Relationships

So far you have seen how to control the mapping of classes and their primitive properties; the final piece is to look at how relationships are mapped. This includes controlling the name of foreign key columns and the name of the join table in many-to-many relationships. Chapter 4 covered a wide variety of conventions and configurations for relationships. Now that you are more familiar with mappings, this section will provide you with additional ways to control particular details of how those relationships are mapped.

Controlling Foreign Keys Included in Your Class

You've seen that a relationship is created by adding navigation properties between two classes. You've also seen that you can optionally include a foreign key property in the dependent class. By default, Code First will use the property name as the name for the column. You saw this back in Chapter 4, when you added the DestinationId to the Lodging class. Code First added a DestinationId column to your database and configured it as a foreign key.

Changing the column name for a foreign key property is exactly the same as changing the column name for any other primitive property. Changing the column name of a foreign key property has no impact on Code First's ability to detect that it is a foreign key. Foreign key detection only considers the property name and not the name of the column it is mapped to.

Let's say you want to change the column name to be destination_id. You can apply the Column annotation directly to the foreign key property:

```
[Column("destination_id")]
public int DestinationId { get; set; }
```

Alternatively, you can change the column name using the Fluent API by adding the following configuration to the LodgingConfiguration class:

```
Property(l => l.DestinationId).HasColumnName("destination_id");
```

Controlling Foreign Keys That Are Created by Code First

As early as Chapter 2, you saw that Code First will create a foreign key column for you when you don't include a foreign key property in your class. You saw this in action with the Lodging class, where a Destination_DestinationId column was added to the database for you. Let's remove the DestinationId foreign key property from the Lodging class so that Code First will automatically generate a foreign key column again (Example 3-10).

 There is one method, DeleteDestinationInMemoryAndDbCascade(), in your console application that uses the Lodging.DestinationId property. You'll want to comment out that method if you plan to run the application with this modification. You will also need to comment out the configuration you just added to rename the column that DestinationId is mapped to.

Example 5-30. Foreign key property commented out

```
public class Lodging
{
  public int LodgingId { get; set; }
  public string Name { get; set; }
  public string Owner { get; set; }
  public decimal MilesFromNearestAirport { get; set; }

  //public int DestinationId { get; set; }
  public Destination Destination { get; set; }
  public List<InternetSpecial> InternetSpecials { get; set; }
  public Nullable<int> PrimaryContactId { get; set; }
  public Person PrimaryContact { get; set; }
  public Nullable<int> SecondaryContactId { get; set; }
  public Person SecondaryContact { get; set; }
}
```

Changing the name of a generated foreign key column is something that can only be done through the Fluent API. In the same way that you used a Map method to control the mapping of a class, you can also use the Map method to control the mapping of a relationship.

Example 5-31 shows how you can add the Map method to the relationship configuration to specify foreign key names.

Example 5-31. Generated foreign key column configured

```
HasRequired(l => l.Destination)
  .WithMany(d => d.Lodgings)
  .Map(c => c.MapKey("destination_id"));
```

Now that you've seen this behavior, go ahead and revert these changes by uncommenting the `DestinationId` foreign key property and removing the above Fluent API configuration. You can also uncomment the `DeleteDestinationInMemoryAndDbCascade` method and the configuration to rename the column that `DestinationId` is mapped to:

```
public int DestinationId { get; set; }
public Destination Destination { get; set; }
```

Controlling generated foreign keys with entity splitting

In "Mapping a Single Entity Across Multiple Tables" on page 99, you saw something called entity splitting. This allows the same class to spread its properties over multiple tables. In these cases you may want to control which table the generated foreign key column gets added to.

By default, the generated foreign key will get added to the first table that you specify in the entity splitting configuration. You can change this by appending a `ToTable` call to the end of your generated foreign key mapping. For example, assume you had split the `Lodging` entity between a `Lodgings` table and a `LodgingInfo` table. If you wanted to place the foreign key to the related destination in the `LodgingInfo` table, you would add a `ToTable` call to the configuration (Example 5-32).

 This code is just provided as an example and won't work with your project if you have been following along.

Example 5-32. Generated foreign key column configured

```
HasRequired(l => l.Destination)
  .WithMany(d => d.Lodgings)
  .Map(c => c.MapKey("destination_id").ToTable("LodgingInfo"));
```

Controlling Many-to-Many Join Tables

In "Exploring Many-to-Many Relationships" on page 78, you saw that introducing a many-to-many relationship between `Activity` and `Trip` resulted in the `ActivityTrips` join table being added to your database (Figure 4-10).

However, in our domain it may make more sense for that table to be called `TripActivities`. Fortunately you can also use the `Map` method when configuring a many-to-many relationship. Let's start by changing the table name. You can do so by adding the configuration shown in Example 5-33 to the `TripConfiguration` class.

Example 5-33. Many-to-many join table name changed

```
HasMany(t => t.Activities)
  .WithMany(a => a.Trips)
  .Map(c => c.ToTable("TripActivities"));
```

The mapping begins by using the `HasMany` and `WithMany` methods to identify the relationship that you are configuring. Once you have identified the relationship, you can use the `Map` method to specify the mapping. Within the mapping, you then use the `ToTable` method to specify the table name. We'll look at some of the other things that can be done inside the Map method next. The join table with the new name applied in the database is shown in Figure 5-12.

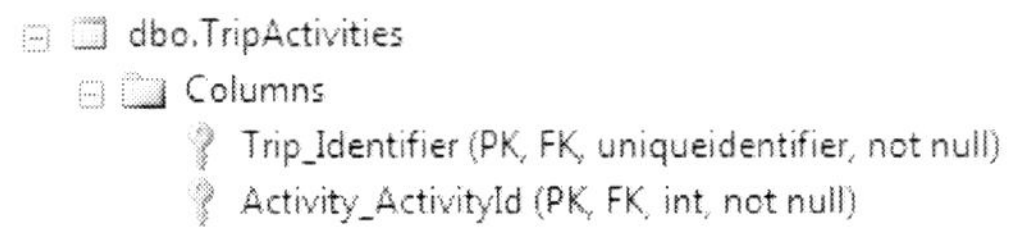

Figure 5-12. Join table renamed

You might also want to tidy up those foreign key names to just be `TripIdentifier` and `ActivityId`. Fortunately, you can also specify column names inside the `Map` method (Example 5-34).

Example 5-34. Changing the many-to-many column names

```
HasMany(t => t.Activities)
  .WithMany(a => a.Trips)
  .Map(c =>
    {
      c.ToTable("TripActivities");
      c.MapLeftKey("TripIdentifier");
      c.MapRightKey("ActivityId");
    });
```

Notice that you use the `MapLeftKey` and `MapRightKey` methods to specify the column names. `MapLeftKey` affects the foreign key column that points to the class being configured. In this case you added the configuration to the `TripConfiguration` class, so `Trip` is the entity being configured. Therefore `Trip` is considered the left entity and `Activity` is considered the right entity. Figure 5-13 shows the join table with its table name and column names changed.

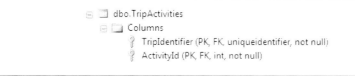

Figure 5-13. Join table columns renamed

Summary

In this chapter you worked with features of Code First that related directly to how your classes and properties map to the database. You've learned how to control the naming of columns, tables, and even schemas. You've seen how to configure classes that map to multiple tables, as well as how to create multiple classes that point to a common table. You've also spent time working with inheritance hierarchies, some of which can only be configured using the Fluent API, and finally you learned how to apply mappings to relationships.

In all, the chapters so far have taught you how to achieve in Code First almost all of the same mapping capabilities that you would have access to if you were working with a EDMX file in the designer. With Code First, you have the ability to plug your domain classes into the Entity Framework without being tied to a designer or an extra model.

CHAPTER 6

Controlling Database Location, Creation Process, and Seed Data

In previous chapters you have seen how convention and configuration can be used to affect the model and the resulting database schema. In this chapter you will see how the convention and configuration concept applies to the database that is used by Code First.

You'll learn how Code First conventions select a database and how you can alter this convention or specify the exact database that your context should use. The topics we cover will help you target other database providers, deploy your application, and perform many other database-related tasks.

You'll also discover how database initializers can be used to control the database creation process and insert seed data into the database. This can be particularly useful when writing automated scenario tests.

Controlling the Database Location

So far you have relied on the Code First convention to select which database the application targets. By default, Code First has created the database on *localhost\SQLEXPRESS* using the fully qualified name of your context class for the database name (i.e., the namespace plus the class name). There will be times when this won't be appropriate and you need to override the convention and tell Code First which database to connect to. You can modify or replace the convention used to select a database using Code First *connection factories*. Alternatively, you can just tell Code First exactly which database to use for a particular context, using the DbContext constructors or your application configuration file.

Code First database creation and initialization works with SQL Azure in the same way that it works with any local database. You can see this in action in "Tutorial: Developing a Windows Azure Data Application Using Code First and SQL Azure" (*http://www.microsoft.com/window sazure/learn/tutorials/road-trip-tutorial/*). Vendors have begun modifying their database providers to support Code First as well. Be sure to check for this support before trying to use Code First with one of the third-party providers.

Controlling Database Location with a Configuration File

The easiest and most definitive way to control the database that your context connects to is via a configuration file. Using the configuration file allows you to bypass all database location–related conventions and specify the exact database you want to use. This approach is particularly useful if you want to change the connection string of your context to point to a production database as you deploy your application.

By default, the connection string that you add to your configuration file should have the same name as your context. The name of the connection string can be either just the type name or the fully qualified type name. In "Controlling Connection String Name with DbContext Constructor" on page 132, you will see how to use a connection string with a name that does not match your context name. Add an *App.config* file to your `BreakAwayConsole` application with a `BreakAwayContext` connection string, as shown in Example 6-1.

Example 6-1. Connection string specified in App.config

```xml
<?xml version="1.0"?>
<configuration>
  <connectionStrings>
    <add name="BreakAwayContext"
         providerName="System.Data.SqlClient"
         connectionString="Server=.\SQLEXPRESS;
           Database=BreakAwayConfigFile;
           Trusted_Connection=true" />
  </connectionStrings>
</configuration>
```

For those familiar with creating connection strings when your application uses an EDMX file, notice that this is not an `EntityConnection` `String` but simply a database connection string. With Code First, you have no need to reference metadata files or the `System.Data.Entity` `Client` namespace.

Modify the `Main` method so that it calls the `InsertDestination` method, as shown in Example 6-2.

Example 6-2. Main method modified to call InsertDestination

```
static void Main()
{
  InsertDestination();
}
```

Run the application, and you will notice that a `BreakAwayConfigFile` database has been created in your local SQL Express instance (Figure 6-1).

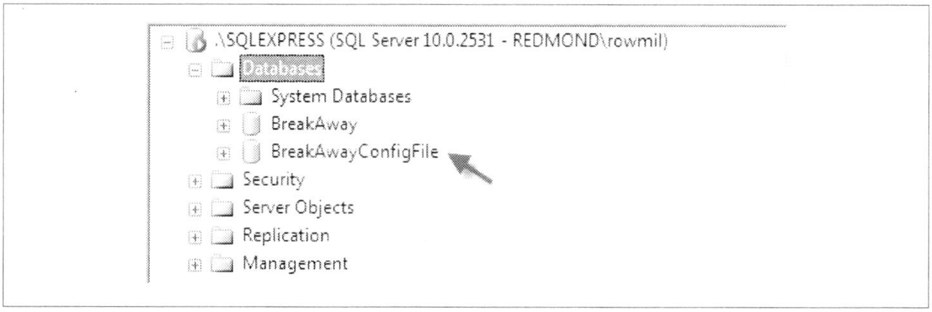

Figure 6-1. New database used based on configuration file setting

Code First matched the `BreakAwayContext` name of your context with the `BreakAwayCon text` connection string in the configuration file. Because an entry was found in the configuration file, the convention for locating a database was not used. The connection string entry could also have been named `DataAccess.BreakAwayContext`, which is the fully qualified name of the context.

Controlling Database Name with DbContext Constructor

You've seen how to set the connection string that your context will use via the configuration file; now let's look at some ways to control the database connection from code. So far you have just used the default constructor on `DbContext`, but there are also a number of other constructors available. Most of these are for more advanced scenarios, which will be covered later in this book, but there are two constructors that allow you to affect the database being connected to.

> If you added a connection string to your configuration file, as shown in the previous section, be sure to remove it before starting this section. Remember that the configuration file overrides everything, including the features you will see in this section.

`DbContext` includes a constructor that takes a single `string` parameter to control the database name. If you use this constructor, the value you supply will be used in place of the fully qualified context name. Add a constructor to `BreakAwayContext` that accepts a string value for the database name and passes it to the base constructor (Example 6-3). Notice that you are also adding a default constructor to ensure that all the existing code from previous chapters continues to work.

Example 6-3. Database name constructor added to context

```
public BreakAwayContext()
{ }

public BreakAwayContext(string databaseName)
  : base(databaseName)
{ }
```

Modify the `Main` method to call a new `SpecifyDatabaseName` method (Example 6-4).

Example 6-4. SpecifyDatabaseName method added to application

```
static void Main()
{
  SpecifyDatabaseName();
}

private static void SpecifyDatabaseName()
{
  using (var context =
    new BreakAwayContext("BreakAwayStringConstructor"))
  {
    context.Destinations.Add(new Destination { Name = "Tasmania" });
    context.SaveChanges();
  }
}
```

This new method uses the constructor you just added to specify a database name. This name is used instead of the fully qualified name of your context. Run the application and you will see that a database named `BreakAwayStringConstructor` has been created in your local SQL Express instance.

Controlling Connection String Name with DbContext Constructor

Earlier in this chapter, you saw that you are able to specify a database to use in the configuration file by adding a connection string with the same name as your context. If you use the `DbContext` constructor that accepts a database name, Entity Framework will look for a connection string whose name matches the database name. In other words, with the default constructor, Entity Framework will look for a connection string named `BreakAwayContext`, but with the constructor used in Example 6-4, it will expect a connection string named `BreakAwayStringConstructor`.

You can also force the context to get its connection string from the configuration file by supplying `name=[connection string name]` to this constructor. This way, you don't need to rely on name matching, since you are explicitly providing a connection string name. If no connection string is found with the specified name, an exception is thrown.

Example 6-5 shows how you can modify the default constructor of BreakAwayContext to ensure that the connection string is always loaded from the configuration file.

If you are following along in Visual Studio, don't make this change, since we are no longer using the config file.

Example 6-5. Constructor defining which connection string should be loaded from App.config

```
public BreakAwayContext()
  :base("name=BreakAwayContext")
{ }
```

Reusing Database Connections

DbContext has another constructor that allows you to supply a DbConnection instance. This can be useful if you have other application logic that works with a DbConnection or if you want to reuse the same connection across multiple contexts. To see this in action, add another constructor to BreakAwayContext that accepts a DbConnection and then passes the DbConnection to the base constructor, as shown in Example 6-6. You'll also notice that you need to specify a value for the contextOwnsConnection. This argument controls whether or not the context should take ownership of the connection. If set to true, the connection will get disposed along with the context. If set to false, your code will need to take care of disposing the connection.

You will need to add a using for the System.Data.Common namespace when you add this new constructor.

Example 6-6. DbConnection constructor added to context

```
public BreakAwayContext(DbConnection connection)
  : base(connection, contextOwnsConnection: false)
{ }
```

Modify the Main method to call a new ReuseDbConnection method, as shown in Example 6-7.

You'll also need to add a using for the System.Data.SqlClient namespace, because the code makes use of the SqlConnection type.

Example 6-7. ReuseDbConnection method added to application

```
static void Main()
{
  ReuseDbConnection();
}

private static void ReuseDbConnection()
{
  var cstr = @"Server=.\SQLEXPRESS;
           Database=BreakAwayDbConnectionConstructor;
           Trusted_Connection=true";

  using (var connection = new SqlConnection(cstr))
  {
    using (var context = new BreakAwayContext(connection))
    {
      context.Destinations.Add(new Destination { Name = "Hawaii" });
      context.SaveChanges();
    }

    using (var context = new BreakAwayContext(connection))
    {
      foreach (var destination in context.Destinations)
      {
        Console.WriteLine(destination.Name);
      }
    }
  }
}
```

The ReuseDbConnection constructs a SqlConnection and then reuses it to construct two separate BreakAwayContext instances. In the example, the SqlConnection is just constructed from a connection string that is defined in code. However, Code First isn't concerned with where you got the connection. You could be getting this connection string from a resource file. You may also be using some existing components that give you an existing DbConnection instance.

Controlling Database Location with Connection Factories

One final option for controlling the database that is used is by swapping out the convention that Code First is using. The convention that Code First uses is available via Database.DefaultConnectionFactory. Connection factories implement the IDbConnectionFactory interface and are responsible for taking the name of a context and creating a DbConnection pointing to the database to be used. Entity Framework includes two connection factory implementations and you can also create your own.

Working with SqlConnectionFactory

The default connection factory for Code First is SqlConnectionFactory. This connection factory will use the SQL Client (System.Data.SqlClient) database provider to connect to a database. The default behavior will select a database on *localhost\SQLEXPRESS* using the fully qualified name of the context type as the database name. Integrated authentication will be used for authenticating with the database server.

You can override parts of this convention by specifying segments of the connection string that are to be set for any connection it creates. These segments are supplied to the constructor of `SqlConnectionFactory` using the same syntax used in connection strings. For example, if you wanted to use a different database server, you can specify the `Server` segment of the connection string:

```
Database.DefaultConnectionFactory =
    new SqlConnectionFactory("Server=MyDatabaseServer");
```

Alternatively, you may want to use different credentials to connect to the database server:

```
Database.DefaultConnectionFactory =
    new SqlConnectionFactory("User=MyUserName;Password=MyPassWord;");
```

Working with SqlCeConnectionFactory

Entity Framework also includes `SqlCeConnectionFactory`, which uses SQL Compact Client to connect to SQL Server Compact Edition databases. By default the database file name matches the fully qualified name of the context class and is created in the | *ApplicationData*| directory.

> For executable applications, |*ApplicationData*| resolves to the directory of the application that is running. For websites, it resolves to an *App_Data* subdirectory of the website's root directory.

Installing SQL Server Compact Edition

Before using SQL Server Compact Edition, you need to install the runtime. The runtime is available as an installer or via NuGet. Install the SqlServerCompact NuGet package to your `BreakAwayConsole` project. You can install the NuGet package by right-clicking on the *References* folder in your `BreakAwayConsole` project and selecting "Add Library Package Reference...." Select "Online" from the left menu and then search for "SqlServerCompact."

Modify the `Main` method, as shown in Example 6-8, to set the `SqlCeConnectionFactory`, and then call the `InsertDestination` method you created back in Chapter 2. The connection factories are included in the `System.Data.Entity.Infrastructure` namespace, so you will need to add a `using` for this. Be sure to read the rest of this section before running the code.

Example 6-8. Changing the default connection factory

```
static void Main()
{
  Database.SetInitializer(
    new DropCreateDatabaseIfModelChanges<BreakAwayContext>());

  Database.DefaultConnectionFactory =
    new SqlCeConnectionFactory("System.Data.SqlServerCe.4.0");

  InsertDestination();
}
```

Notice that you need to specify a string that identifies the database provider to use (known as the *provider invariant name*). This string is chosen by the provider writer to uniquely identify the provider. Most providers keep the same identifier between versions, but SQL Compact uses a different identifier for each version. This is because SQL Compact providers are not backwards-compatible (you can't use, for example, the 4.0 provider to connect to a 3.5 database). The SqlCeConnectionFactory needs to know what version of the provider to use, so it requires you to supply this string.

If you want to test out this code, you will need to make a small change to your model. Back in Chapter 3, we configured Trip.Identifier to be a database-generated key. Identifier is a GUID property and SQL Server had no problem generating values for us. SQL Compact, however, isn't able to generate values for GUID columns. If you want to run the application, remove either the Data Annotation or Fluent API call that configures Trip.Identifier as database-generated.

Once you've made this change, you can run the application and you will notice that a *DataAccess.BreakawayContext.sdf* file is created in the output directory of your application (Figure 6-2). Now that you've seen SQL Compact in action, go ahead and re-enable the configuration to make Trip.Identifier database-generated.

Writing a custom connection factory

So far you have seen the connection factories that are included in Entity Framework, but you can also write your own by implementing the IDbConnectionFactory interface. The interface is simple and contains a single CreateConnection method that accepts the context name and returns a DbConnection.

In this section, you'll build a custom connection factory that is very similar to SqlConnectionFactory, except it will just use the context class name, rather than its fully qualified name for the database. You'll also build this custom factory so that it will remove the word Context if it's found in the context name.

Start by adding a CustomConnectionFactory class to your DataAccess project (Example 6-9).

Figure 6-2. SQL Server Compact file created in output directory

Example 6-9. Custom connection factory implementation

```csharp
using System.Data.Common;
using System.Data.Entity.Infrastructure;
using System.Data.SqlClient;
using System.Linq;

namespace DataAccess
{
  public class CustomConnectionFactory : IDbConnectionFactory
  {
    public DbConnection CreateConnection(
      string nameOrConnectionString)
    {
      var name = nameOrConnectionString
        .Split('.').Last()
        .Replace("Context", string.Empty);

      var builder = new SqlConnectionStringBuilder
      {
        DataSource = @".\SQLEXPRESS",
        InitialCatalog = name,
```

```
        IntegratedSecurity = true,
        MultipleActiveResultSets = true
      };

      return new SqlConnection(builder.ToString());
    }
  }
}
```

The CustomConnectionFactory implementation uses the Split method to take the section of the context name after the final period to use for the database name. It then replaces any instances of the Context word with an empty string. Then it uses SqlConnection StringBuilder to create a connection string that is then used to construct a SqlConnection.

With this method in place, you can modify the Main method to make use of the custom connection factory you just created (Example 6-10). You do so by setting the Custom ConnectionFactory as the DefaultConnectionFactory before other code, which will be using a context.

Example 6-10. Default connection factory set to new custom factory

```
static void Main()
{
  Database.SetInitializer(
    new DropCreateDatabaseIfModelChanges<BreakAwayContext>());

  Database.DefaultConnectionFactory = new CustomConnectionFactory();

  InsertDestination();
}
```

Run the application and you will see that a new "BreakAway" database is created on the local SQL Express instance (Figure 6-3). The custom factory you just created has removed the namespace from the database name and also stripped the word "Context" from the end.

Figure 6-3. BreakAway database created on local SQL Express

Working with Database Initialization

In Chapter 2, you saw that an initializer can be set for a context type using the `Database.SetInitializer` method. The initializer you set allowed the database to be dropped and recreated whenever the model changed:

```
Database.SetInitializer(
    new DropCreateDatabaseIfModelChanges<BreakAwayContext>());
```

Initialization involves two main steps. First, the model is created in memory using the Code First conventions and configuration discussed in previous chapters. Second, the database that will be used to store data is initialized using the database initializer that has been set. By default, this initialization will use the model that Code First calculated to create a database schema for you. Initialization will occur one time per application instance; in .NET Framework applications, the application instance is also referred to as an `AppDomain`. Initialization is triggered the first time that the context is used. Initialization occurs lazily, so creating an instance of the context is not enough to cause initialization to happen. An operation that requires the model must be performed, such as querying or adding entities.

> The initialization process is thread-safe, so multiple threads in the same `AppDomain` can use the same context type. `DbContext` itself is not thread-safe, so a given instance of the context type must only be used in a single thread.

Controlling When Database Initialization Occurs

There are situations where you may want to control when initialization occurs, rather than leaving it to happen automatically the first time your context is used in an application instance. Initialization can be triggered using the `DbContext.Database.Initialize` method. This method takes a single boolean parameter named `force`. Supplying `false` will cause the initialization to occur only if it hasn't yet been triggered in the current `AppDomain`. Remember that running the initializer once per `AppDomain` is the default behavior. Setting `force` to `true` will cause the initialization process to run even if it has already occurred in the current `AppDomain`. Because the context also triggers initialization, this code needs to run prior to the context being used in the `AppDomain`.

Why would you want to manually trigger database initialization? You may want to manually trigger initialization so that any errors that occur during model creation and database initialization can be caught and processed in a single place. Another reason to force initialization to occur would be to front-load the cost of creating a large and/or complex model.

Let's see this in action. Modify the `Main` method, adding in code to force database initialization to occur, and handle any exceptions that occur as a result of building the model (Example 6-11).

Example 6-11. Main method updated to process initialization errors

```
static void Main()
{
  Database.SetInitializer(
    new DropCreateDatabaseIfModelChanges<BreakAwayContext>());

  using (var context = new BreakAwayContext())
  {
    try
    {
      context.Database.Initialize(force: false);
    }
    catch (Exception ex)
    {
      Console.WriteLine("Initialization Failed...");
      Console.WriteLine(ex.Message);
    }
  }
}
```

Now we'll make a change that will cause initialization to fail by asking Code First to map a numeric property to a string column. Doing this will cause the model creation process to fail before Code First even tries to create the database schema.

Modify `Activity` and add in a `Column` annotation that specifies a `varchar` data type to be used for the `ActivityId` property (Example 6-12).

Example 6-12. ActivityId mapped to an incompatible database type

```
public class Activity
{
  [Column(TypeName = "varchar")]
  public int ActivityId { get; set; }
  [Required, MaxLength(50)]
  public string Name { get; set; }
  public List<Trip> Trips { get; set; }
}
```

Run the application and the program will display the exception informing us that the data type that was specified is not valid because of the invalid cast:

Initialization Failed...

Schema specified is not valid. Errors:

(122,12) : error 2019: Member Mapping specified is not valid. The type 'Edm.Int32[Nullable=False,DefaultValue=]' of member 'ActivityId' in type 'DataAccess.Activity' is not compatible with 'SqlServer.varchar[Nullable=False,DefaultValue=,MaxLength=8000,Unicode=False,FixedLength=False,StoreGeneratedPattern=Identity]' of member 'ActivityId' in type 'CodeFirstDatabaseSchema.Activity'.

(146,10) : error 2019: Member Mapping specified is not valid. The type 'Edm.Int32[Nullable=False,DefaultValue=]' of member 'ActivityId' in type 'DataAccess.Activity' is not compatible with 'SqlServer.varchar[Nullable=False,DefaultValue=,Max-

Length=8000,Unicode=False,FixedLength=False]' of member 'Activity_ActivityId' in type 'CodeFirstDatabaseSchema.ActivityTrip'.

Remove the annotation you just added to `DestinationId` and run the application again. This time there will be no error.

Switching Off Database Initialization Completely

Of course, not every scenario calls for the database to be automatically initialized, and Entity Framework caters to these situations, too. For example, if you are mapping to an existing database, you probably want Code First to error if it can't connect to the database, rather than trying to magically create one for you. You can switch off initialization by passing null to `Database.SetInitializer`:

```
Database.SetInitializer(null);
```

When the initializer is set to null, `DbContext.Database.Initialize` can still be used to force model creation to occur.

Database Initializers Included in Entity Framework

You'll notice that `Database.SetInitializer` accepts an instance of `IDatabaseInitializer<TContext>`. There are three implementations of this interface included in Entity Framework. These implementations are abstract, so you can derive from them and customize the behavior. We'll walk through creating your own implementation a little later on.

CreateDatabaseIfNotExists
> This is the default initializer that is set for all contexts unless `Database.SetInitializer` is used to specify an alternative initializer. This is the safest initializer, as the database will never be dropped automatically, causing data loss. We saw in Chapter 2 that if the model is changed from when the database was created, an exception is thrown during initialization:
>
>> The model backing the "BreakAwayContext" context has changed since the database was created. Either manually delete/update the database, or call `Database.SetInitializer` with an `IDatabaseInitializer` instance. For example, the `DropCreateDatabaseIfModelChanges` strategy will automatically delete and recreate the database, and optionally seed it with new data.
>
> Because this is the default initializer, you shouldn't need to set it, but if you find a need to you can use the following code:
>
> ```
> Database.SetInitializer(
>   new CreateDatabaseIfNotExists<BreakAwayContext>());
> ```

DropCreateDatabaseWhenModelChanges
> You've seen this initializer used throughout the previous chapters to make sure the database always matches the current model. If Code First detects that the model

and database do not match, the database will be dropped and recreated so that it matches the current model. This is useful during development, but you obviously wouldn't want to use this when deploying your application, as it will result in data loss. We've already seen the code required to set this initializer:

```
Database.SetInitializer(
    new DropCreateDatabaseIfModelChanges<BreakAwayContext>());
```

DropCreateDatabaseAlways

This initializer will drop and recreate the database regardless of whether the model matches the database or not. At first glance, you may wonder why you would ever want to do that. If you are writing integration tests that exercise your whole application stack, it can be useful to have a way to reset the database to a well-known state before running a test. Modify the Main method as shown in Example 6-13 to run some code that could represent a test that uses your application to insert a single Destination.

Example 6-13. Implementation of a pseudo integration test

```
static void Main()
{
  Database.SetInitializer(
    new DropCreateDatabaseAlways<BreakAwayContext>());
  RunTest();
}

private static void RunTest()
{
  using (var context = new BreakAwayContext())
  {
    context.Destinations.Add(new Destination { Name = "Fiji" });
    context.SaveChanges();
  }

  using (var context = new BreakAwayContext())
  {
    if (context.Destinations.Count() == 1)
    {
      Console.WriteLine(
        "Test Passed: 1 destination saved to database");
    }
    else
    {
      Console.WriteLine(
        "Test Failed: {0} destinations saved to database",
        context.Destinations.Count());
    }
  }
}
```

Because the initializer is set to drop and recreate the database each time, you know that the database will be empty before the test starts. You won't always want the database to be empty before running integration tests, and we'll look at seeding data a little later on. Go ahead and run the application, and we will see that the test passes.

So far we have just executed a single test, but normally there would be multiple tests required to test an application. Update the `Main` method so that it runs the same test twice in a row (Example 6-14).

Example 6-14. Main updated to run the test twice

```
static void Main(string[] args)
{
  Database.SetInitializer(
    new DropCreateDatabaseAlways<BreakAwayContext>());

  RunTest();
  RunTest();
}
```

Run the application, and you will see that the first execution of the test method will succeed but the second one will fail, stating that there are two destinations in the database. The second test is failing because the data from the first execution is still in the database. This is happening because `AppDomain` only runs the initializer once by default.

Earlier in this chapter, you learned that you can use `Database.Initialize` to force initialization to occur, even if has already happened in the current `AppDomain`. Modify the `RunTest` method to include a call to `Database.Initialize` with force set to true to ensure the database is reset before each test (Example 6-15). Run the application again and you will see both tests now pass. The database is getting dropped and recreated in the well-known state before each execution.

Example 6-15. RunTest updated to force initialization

```
static void RunTest()
{
  using (var context = new BreakAwayContext())
  {
    context.Database.Initialize(force: true);

    context.Destinations.Add(new Destination { Name = "Fiji" });
    context.SaveChanges();
  }

  using (var context = new BreakAwayContext())
  {
    if (context.Destinations.Count() == 1)
    {
      Console.WriteLine(
        "Test Passed: 1 destination saved to database");
    }
    else
    {
      Console.WriteLine(
        "Test Failed: {0} destinations saved to database",
```

```
            context.Destinations.Count());
      }
    }
  }
}
```

Dropping and recreating the database is an easy way to start each test with a well-known state, but it can be expensive if you are running a lot of integration tests. Consider using `System.Transactions.TransactionScope` as a way to avoid changes being permanently saved to the database during each test.

Creating a Custom Database Initializer

So far, you have used the initializers that are included in the Entity Framework API. There may be times when the initialization logic that you want doesn't align with any of the included initializers. Fortunately `Database.SetInitializer` accepts the `IDataba seInitializer` interface, which you can implement to provide your own logic.

 As well as writing your own custom initializers, you can also find initializers that other people have created. One example of this is available in the `EFCodeFirst.CreateTablesOnly` NuGet package. This initializer will allow you to drop and create the tables in an existing database, rather than dropping and creating the actual database itself. This is particularly useful if you are targeting a hosted database where you don't have permission to drop or create the entire database.

There could be any number of reasons you want to implement your own initializer. We are going to look at a simple scenario where the developer will be prompted before the database is dropped and recreated. The `Database` property exposes a variety of methods to interact with the database such as checking to see if it exists, creating it, or dropping it. The three initializers that are included in the API contain logic that leverages these methods. You can combine the methods in logic in your own class. That's what you'll do in this next example. Add the `PromptForDropCreateDatabaseWhenModelChages` class to your DataAccess project (Example 6-16).

Example 6-16. Custom initializer

```
using System;
using System.Data.Entity;

namespace DataAccess
{
  public class PromptForDropCreateDatabaseWhenModelChages<TContext>
    : IDatabaseInitializer<TContext>
    where TContext : DbContext
  {
    public void InitializeDatabase(TContext context)
    {
      // If the database exists and matches the model
```

```
    // there is nothing to do
    var exists = context.Database.Exists();
    if (exists && context.Database.CompatibleWithModel(true))
    {
      return;
    }

    // If the database exists and doesn't match the model
    // then prompt for input
    if (exists)
    {
      Console.WriteLine
        ("Existing database doesn't match the model!");
      Console.Write
        ("Do you want to drop and create the database? (Y/N): ");
      var res = Console.ReadKey();
      Console.WriteLine();
      if (!String.Equals(
        "Y",
        res.KeyChar.ToString(),
        StringComparison.OrdinalIgnoreCase))
      {
        return;
      }

      context.Database.Delete();
    }

    // Database either didn't exist or it didn't match
    // the model and the user chose to delete it
    context.Database.Create();
  }
 }
}
```

The PromptForDropCreateDatabaseWhenModelChages class implements a single Initiali
zeDatabase method. First, it checks if the database exists and matches the current
model. If it does, there is nothing else to be done and the initializer returns. If the
database exists but doesn't match the current model, you will be prompted to see if
you want to drop and create the database. If you decide not to recreate the database,
the initializer returns and Entity Framework will attempt to run against the existing
database schema. If you do decide to recreate the database, the existing database is
dropped. The final line of code simply creates the database and is only reached if the
database didn't exist or if we chose to recreate the database.

The custom initializer now needs to be registered with the Entity Framework; modify
the Main method to take care of this (Example 6-17). You'll notice that we're also updating Main so that it calls the InsertDestination method that we wrote back in
Chapter 2.

Example 6-17. Custom initializer registered in Main

```
static void Main()
{
  Database.SetInitializer(new
    PromptForDropCreateDatabaseWhenModelChages<BreakAwayContext>());
  InsertDestination();
}
```

Let's go ahead and change the model so that it no longer matches the database. Modify the `Destination` class by adding a `MaxLength` annotation to the `Name` property:

```
[MaxLength(200)]
public string Name { get; set; }
```

Now run the application, and you will be prompted, asking if you want to drop and create the database. Answer no (`N`) to tell our custom initializer to leave the database alone this time. You'll notice that the application still completes successfully. This is because the changes you made don't prevent Entity Framework from being able to use the current model to access the out-of-date database schema. Entity Framework expects that `Destination` names should be 200 characters or less. Since the database didn't change, it doesn't enforce max length, so it's happy with the insert statement that Entity Framework is sending to the database.

Now let's make a change that will affect the insert statement. Modify the `Destination` class to include a new `TravelWarnings` property:

```
public string TravelWarnings { get; set; }
```

Run the application again. As before, you'll be prompted, asking if you want to drop and create the database. Select not to recreate the database again, and this time you will get a `DbUpdateException`. You'll need to drill through the inner exceptions to find the actual cause of the error (Figure 6-4).

The inner exception of the top-level exception is an `UpdateException`, and the inner exception of that is a `SqlException`. The `SqlException` finally has the message that explains what happened: "`Invalid column name 'TravelWarnings'`." The problem is that Entity Framework is trying to execute the SQL shown in Example 6-18, but the `Trav elWarnings` column doesn't exist in the database.

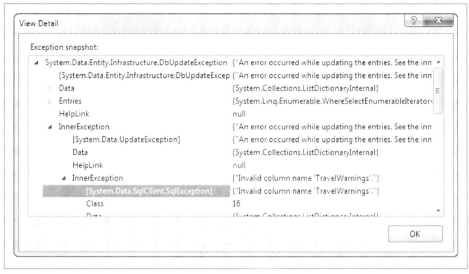

Figure 6-4. Exception while inserting a Destination

Example 6-18. Invalid SQL being executed

```
insert [dbo].[Destinations]([Name], [Country], [Description],
            [TravelWarnings], [Photo])
values (@0, @1, @2, null, null)
select [DestinationId]
from [dbo].[Destinations]
where @@ROWCOUNT > 0 and [DestinationId] = scope_identity()
```

Run the application again, but this time select to drop and recreate the database when prompted. The application will now execute successfully.

Setting Database Initializers from a Configuration File

Setting initializers in code is an easy way to get started while developing, but when it's time to deploy your application, you probably want to have an easier way to set them without modifying code. It's highly unlikely you want to deploy your application with the DropCreateDatabaseIfModelChanges initializer set in production! Add an appSet tings section to the config file of your BreakAwayConsole project that includes the ini-tializer setting shown in Example 6-19.

Example 6-19. Initializer set in configuration file

```
<?xml version="1.0"?>
<configuration>
  <appSettings>
    <add key="DatabaseInitializerForType DataAccess.BreakAwayContext, DataAccess"
      value="System.Data.Entity.DropCreateDatabaseIfModelChanges`1
          [[DataAccess.BreakAwayContext, DataAccess]], EntityFramework" />
```

```
    </appSettings>
</configuration>
```

 The example includes a line break for formatting, but you should remove the line break in your *App.config* file. The value needs to be on a
single line for the setting to work.

There is a lot going on in the line of configuration, so let's break down how it is struc-
tured. The key section always starts off with DatabaseInitializerForType followed by
a space, then the assembly qualified name of the context that the initializer is being set
for. In our case that is DataAccess.BreakAwayContext, DataAccess, which simply means
the DataAccess.BreakAwayContext type that is defined in the DataAccess assembly. The
value section is the assembly qualified name of the database initializer to be used. It
looks complex because we are using a generic type; we are setting
DropCreateDatabaseIfModelChanges<BreakAwayContext> defined in the EntityFrame
work assembly.

Also modify the Main method so that it no longer sets an initializer in code:

```
static void Main()
{
    InsertDestination();
}
```

Now make a change to the model so that you can test that the entry in our configuration
file is being used. Modify the Destination class to include a new ClimateInfo property:

```
public string ClimateInfo { get; set; }
```

Run the application, and you will see that the database gets dropped and recreated with
the new ClimateInfo column.

Now if you want to deploy your application, you may want to change the initializer to
CreateDatabaseIfNotExists so that you never incur automatic data loss. You may also
be working with a DBA who is going to create the database for you. If the database is
being created outside of the Code First workflow, you will want to switch off database
initialization altogether. You can do that by changing the configuration file to specify
Disabled for the initializer (Example 6-20).

Example 6-20. Initializer disabled in configuration file

```
<?xml version="1.0"?>
<configuration>
  <appSettings>
    <add key="DatabaseInitializerForType DataAccess.BreakAwayContext, DataAccess"
        value="Disabled" />
  </appSettings>
</configuration>
```

Now that we've explored setting database initializers in a config file, be sure to remove any settings that you have added.

Using Database Initializers to Seed Data

In this chapter, you have seen how database initializers can be used to control how and when Code First creates the database. So far, the database that Code First creates has always been empty, but there are situations where you may want Code First to create your database with some seed data. You may have some lookup tables that have a predefined set of data, such as Gender or Country. You may just want some sample data in your database while you are working locally so that you can see how your application behaves.

Another scenario where seed data can be useful is running integration tests. In the previous section, we wrote a test that relied on an empty database; now let's write one that relies on a database containing some well-known data.

Let's start by writing the test you are going to run. Modify the `Main` method to run a test that verifies there is a `Destination` entry for "Great Barrier Reef" in our database (Example 6-21). Be sure you have removed any settings you added to the config file in the previous section.

Example 6-21. Implementation of pseudo test reliant on seed data

```
static void Main()
{
  Database.SetInitializer(
    new DropCreateDatabaseAlways<BreakAwayContext>());
  GreatBarrierReefTest();
}

static void GreatBarrierReefTest()
{
  using (var context = new BreakAwayContext())
  {
    var reef = from destination in context.Destinations
               where destination.Name == "Great Barrier Reef"
               select destination;

    if (reef.Count() == 1)
    {
      Console.WriteLine(
        "Test Passed: 1 'Great Barrier Reef' destination found");
    }
    else
    {
      Console.WriteLine(
        "Test Failed: {0} 'Great Barrier Reef' destinations found",
        context.Destinations.Count());
    }
```

```
    }
}
```

Run the application, and you will see that the test fails, stating that there are no entries for "Great Barrier Reef" in the database. This makes sense, because you set the Drop CreateDatabaseAlways initializer, which will create and empty the database for us.

What the test really needs is a variation of DropCreateDatabaseAlways that will insert some seed data after it has created the database. The three initializers that are included in the Entity Framework are not sealed, meaning you can create your own initializer that derives from one of the included ones. All three of the included initializers also include a Seed method that is virtual (Overridable in Visual Basic), meaning it can be overridden. The seed method has an empty implementation, but the initializers will call it at the appropriate time to insert seed data that you provide.

To check out this feature, add a DropCreateBreakAwayWithSeedData class to your Data-Access project. The key to providing the seed data is to override the initializer's Seed method, as shown in Example 6-22.

Example 6-22. Initializer with seed data implemented

```
using System.Data.Entity;
using Model;

namespace DataAccess
{
  public class DropCreateBreakAwayWithSeedData :
    DropCreateDatabaseAlways<BreakAwayContext>
  {
    protected override void Seed(BreakAwayContext context)
    {
      context.Destinations.Add(new Destination
          { Name = "Great Barrier Reef" });
      context.Destinations.Add(new Destination
          { Name = "Grand Canyon" });
    }
  }
}
```

> Notice that there is no call to context.SaveChanges() at the end of the Seed method in Example 6-24. The base Seed method will call that for you after the code in your custom method has been executed. If you let Visual Studio's editor auto-implement the override method for you, it will include a call to base.Seed(context). You can leave that in if you like, but be sure to let it be the last line of code in the method.

Now that you have created an initializer that will insert seed data, it needs to be registered with Entity Framework so that it will be used. This is achieved in same way that we registered the included initializers earlier—via the Database.SetInitializer method.

Modify the `Main` method so that `DropCreateBreakAwayWithSeedData` is registered (Example 6-23).

Example 6-23. Initializer with seed data is registered

```
static void Main()
{
  Database.SetInitializer(new DropCreateBreakAwayWithSeedData());
  GreatBarrierReefTest();
}
```

Run the application again, and the test will pass this time because Code First is now using `DropCreateBreakAwayWithSeedData` to initialize the database. Because this initializer derives from `DropCreateDatabaseAlways`, it will drop the database and recreate and empty one. The `Seed` method that you overrode will then be called and the seed data you specified is inserted into the newly created database each time.

 The `Seed` method in Example 6-24 is a great first look at seeding the database but somewhat simplistic. You can insert various types of data and related data as well. For an example of an efficient LINQ method used to insert entire graphs of related data in `Seed`, check out my blog post, Seeding a Database with Code First (*http://thedatafarm.com/blog/data-access/seeding-a-database-with-ef4-code-first*).

Using Database Initialization to Further Affect Database Schema

In addition to seeding a database when Code First creates it, you may want to affect the database in ways that can't be done with configurations or data seeding. For example, you may want to create an `Index` on the `Name` field of the `Lodgings` table to speed up searches by name.

You can achieve this by calling the `DbContext.Database.ExecuteSqlCommand` method along with the SQL to create the index inside the `Seed` method. Example 6-24 shows the modified `Seed` method that forces this `Index` to be created before the data is inserted.

Example 6-24. Using the ExecuteSqlCommand to add an Index to the database

```
protected override void Seed(BreakAwayContext context)
{
  context.Database.ExecuteSqlCommand
   ("CREATE INDEX IX_Lodgings_Name ON Lodgings (Name)");
  context.Destinations.Add(new Destination
      { Name = "Great Barrier Reef" });
  context.Destinations.Add(new Destination
      { Name = "Grand Canyon" });
}
```

Summary

In this chapter you saw how Code First interacts with the database by default, and how you can override this default behavior. You've learned how to control the database that Code First connects to and how that database is initialized. You've also seen how database initializers can be used in scenario tests to insert seed data into the database as it is initialized.

Throughout this book, you have seen how Code First creates a model based on your domain classes and configuration. You've then seen how Code First locates and initializes the database that the model will be used to access. In the next chapter, you will learn about some advanced concepts that you probably won't use regularly, but you may find useful from time to time.

CHAPTER 7

Advanced Concepts

The Code First modeling functionality that you have seen so far should be enough to get you up and running with most applications. However, Code First also includes some more advanced functionality that you may require as your needs advance. Throughout this book you've seen Code First's conventions in action, but if there are one or more conventions you don't like, Code First allows you to remove them. You may also want to get rid of that `EdmMetadata` table Code First is adding to your database. Code First caches its model by default, and it's possible to override that behavior to solve problems like targeting multiple database providers in the same application instance. This chapter will cover these topics and more.

Mapping to Nontable Database Objects

So far you have used Code First to map to tables, whether you are generating a database or mapping to tables in an existing database. But databases support many other types of objects, including stored procedures and views.

As of Entity Framework 4.2, Code First only has built-in support for tables, meaning that it is only capable of generating schemas that contain tables. Therefore, if you are using Code First to generate your database, you are restricted to tables.

However, if you are mapping to an existing database, you may have views, stored procedures, and other objects in the database you are mapping to. Let's take a look at how we can interact with those.

> You have the option of manually editing the database schema after Code First has created it. If you do manually edit the database to include nontable objects, you can apply the same techniques discussed in this section.
>
> The Entity Framework team has indicated that they plan to add support for mapping to other database objects in future releases.

Mapping to Updatable Views

In some cases you may want to simply map an entity to a view rather than a table. For example, you may be mapping to a database that has a very large and confusing schema. To simplify things, the database might contain a view that exposes the data for your entity with more comprehensible column names. If the view is updatable, you can use the Entity Framework to insert, update, and delete data as well as selecting it. Fortunately, most databases, including SQL Server, use the same SQL syntax for interacting with views as they do for tables. This means you can simply "lie" to Code First and tell it that the view is a table. You do this by using the same configuration you use for naming tables.

 Curious about updatable views? Check out SQL Server's "CREATE VIEW (Transact-SQL)" topic (*http://msdn.microsoft.com/en-us/library/ms187956.aspx*) on MSDN. There's a helpful explanation about what makes a view updatable.

For example, perhaps you want the `Destination` data to come from an updateable view called `my_destination_view` rather than a table. You can use the `Table` annotation to specify the view name:

```
[Table("my_detination_view")]
public class Destination
```

Alternatively, you can use the `ToTable` method from the Fluent API to map to the view:

```
modelBuilder.Entity<Destination>().ToTable("my_detination_view");
```

Using Views to Populate Objects

Not all scenarios call for mapping an entity directly to an updateable view. You may find yourself wanting to leave a class mapped to a table but to have the ability to use a view to retrieve a set of those classes in a particular scenario. For example, let's assume that you want to leave `Destination` mapped to the `Destinations` table, but in one area of your application you want to load all the destinations from the `TopTenDestinations` view. You can use the `SqlQuery` method on `DbSet` to load entities based on some SQL that you write:

```
var destinations = context.Destinations
    .SqlQuery("SELECT * FROM dbo.TopTenDestinations");
```

In the above code we are using a SQL statement that bypasses Entity Framework to get back the desired `Destination` objects. The good thing is that once those objects are retrieved from the database, they are treated exactly the same as objects that were loaded any other way. This means you still get change tracking, lazy loading, and other `DbContext` features for the `Destination` objects that were loaded.

The `SqlQuery` method relies on an exact match between the column names in the result set of the query you wrote and the names of the properties in your object. Because the `Destination` class contains `DestinationId`, `Name`, and other properties, the view must return columns with these same names. If the view does not have the same column names as the properties on your class, you will need to alias the columns in your select statement.

For example, let's say that your `TopTenDestinations` view uses `Id` instead of `DestinationId` for the primary key name. In SQL Server, you can use the AS word to alias the `Id` column from the view as the `DestinationId` column that Entity Framework is expecting, as you can see in Example 7-1.

Example 7-1. Querying a database view from a DbSet

```
var destinations = context.Destinations
  .SqlQuery(@"SELECT
                Id AS DestinationId,
                Name,
                Country,
                Description,
                Photo
             FROM dbo.TopTenDestinations");
```

Note that the column-to-property name matching does not take any mapping into account. For example, if you had mapped the `DestinationId` property to a column called `Id` in the `Destinations` table, the `SqlQuery` method would not use this mapping. The `SqlQuery` method always attempts the column-to-property matching based on property name. Therefore, the column in the result set would still need to be called `DestinationId`.

Using Views to Populate Nonmodel Objects

The two techniques we have looked at so far allow you to use a view to populate a set of objects that are part of your model. Once these objects are created, they are tracked by the context and any changes will be written back to the database. You may find yourself wanting to get the results of a view back into a read-only set of objects. The results of the view may combine data from multiple tables and therefore can't be mapped directly to an entity that is part of your model.

For example, you may have a view called `DestinationSummaryView` that combines data from the `Destinations` and `Lodgings` tables. This view may have `DestinationId`, `Name`, `LodgingCount`, and `ResortCount` columns. These columns don't match any of the entities in the BAGA model, but it would be great to be able to get the results back into a purpose-built object that you can then use in your application.

The `DestinationSummary` class might look something like Example 7-2.

Example 7-2. DestinationSummary implementation

```
public class DestinationSummary
{
  public int DestinationId { get; set; }
  public string Name { get; set; }
  public int LodgingCount { get; set; }
  public int ResortCount { get; set; }
}
```

Because the class isn't part of the BAGA model, you can't use a `DbSet` to query for results. Instead, you use the `SqlQuery` method on `DbContext.Database` as follows:

```
var summary = context.Database.SqlQuery<DestinationSummary>(
  "SELECT * FROM dbo.DestinationSummaryView");
```

In response, Entity Framework will run the SQL that you supplied to access the `Desti nationSummaryView` view. It will then take these results and try to match the column names up with the property names of the `DestinationSummary` class that you specified in the generic argument of `SqlQuery`. Because the column and property names match, we will get the results of the query in a collection of `DestinationSummary` objects.

Because we didn't go through a `DbSet` as we did in Example 7-1, the `DestinationSum mary` objects that are created are not tracked by the context. Therefore, if you change any of the properties, Entity Framework will not pay any attention to those changes any time `SaveChanges` is called.

Working with Stored Procedures

Code First does not have any support for mapping Insert, Update, and Delete statements for your classes directly to stored procedures, as you are able to do in the designer.

> The Entity Framework team has indicated that this is a common request they hear from customers and something they will likely add in a future release.

Using the same techniques you just saw for working with views, you can also use stored procedures to fetch results from the database. For example, let's say you have a `Get TopTenDestinations` stored procedure that takes a single parameter to specify in which country to look for destinations. You can use the `SqlQuery` method on `DbSet` to execute this procedure:

```
var country = "Australia";
var destinations = context.Destinations
  .SqlQuery("dbo.GetTopTenDestinations @p0", country);
```

Notice that SqlQuery accepts parameters. See the sidebar "SqlQuery Parameters to Prevent SQL Injection" on page 157 for more information.

As you saw above with views, you can also use the `DbContext.Database.SqlQuery` method to get back results from stored procedures that don't match an entity in your model. Let's assume you have a `GetDestinationSummary` stored procedure and you want to get the results in a collection of the `DestinationSummary` class you saw back in Example 7-2. Let's also say this stored procedure takes two parameters—one for the country and the other for some keywords:

```
var country = "Australia";
var keyWords = "Beach, Sun";
var destinations = context.Database.SqlQuery<DestinationSummary>(
    "dbo.GetDestinationSummary @p0, @p1", country, keyWords);
```

In the above code, you can see that we're using index-based naming for parameters. As noted in the sidebar, Entity Framework will wrap these parameters up as `DbParameter` objects for you to avoid any SQL injection issues. The column names in the result returned by the stored procedure will be matched with the property names on `DestinationSummary`. Because `DestinationSummary` isn't part of the BAGA model, the results are not tracked and any changes will not be pushed back to the database.

SqlQuery Parameters to Prevent SQL Injection

The `SqlQuery` method allows you to specify parameters. Entity Framework will take care of wrapping these into `DbParameter` objects to help prevent against SQL injection attacks. You use a `@p` prefix for parameters followed by an integer index. Entity Framework will then match these indexes up with the list of parameters you provide after the query string. As with the view-based example you saw earlier, the results of the query are tracked by the context and behave the same as results of any other query.

Removing Conventions

In previous chapters you have seen that Code First includes a set of conventions that help build your model. You've seen how you can supplement or override what the conventions do using Data Annotations or the Fluent API. One other option you have is to switch off one or more of the default conventions.

Each Code First convention is implemented as a class in the `System.Data.Entity.ModelConfiguration.Conventions` namespace. Code First currently only allows you to remove one or more of the included conventions.

 The ability to write your own conventions was included in a preview of Code First. However, the Entity Framework team removed this functionality because they felt that they didn't have time to polish the design and get to the appropriate quality level without holding up the much-awaited release of Code First. It's likely this feature will become available again in a future release.

A full list of the Code First conventions that can be removed and a description of what each convention does is available at *http://msdn.microsoft.com/en-us/library/gg696316(v=VS.103).aspx*. The complete list of conventions is also shown in Figure 7-1.

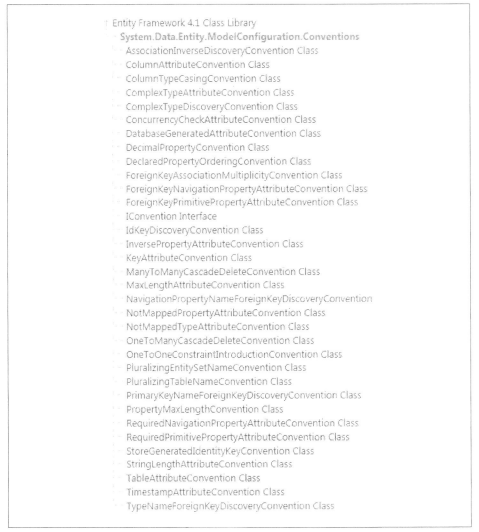

Figure 7-1. Code First conventions as listed in the MSDN library

While you can remove any of the conventions listed in Figure 7-1, we'll use just one— OneToManyCascadeDelete—to demonstrate how to go about this process. This convention adds a cascade delete rule to all required relationships.

While you could just override the cascade behavior for every required relationship, if you have a lot of relationships, it may make more sense just to disable the convention altogether.

Switching off conventions is done in the `OnModelCreating` method on your context via the `DbModelBuilder.Conventions.Remove` method. Add the following line of code to `OnModelCreating` in your `BreakAwayContext` class:

```
modelBuilder.Conventions.Remove<OneToManyCascadeDeleteConvention>();
```

The model contains a required relationship between `Lodging` and `Destination`. Up until now, Code First has been automatically adding a cascade delete rule to this relationship. With the new code in place, run the application so that the database gets recreated and this cascade delete will be removed from this relationship in the model and in the database (Figure 7-2). It will also disappear from any other required relationships that may exist.

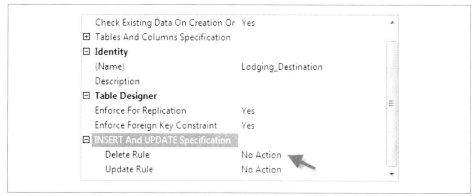

Figure 7-2. Cascade delete off between Lodging and Destination

After switching off the conventions, you may decide that you want to reintroduce cascade delete behavior on some of the relationships. You can do this using the Fluent API as described back in Chapter 4.

In the BAGA model, it makes sense for us to have cascade delete enabled on required relationships, so go ahead and re-enable the `OneToManyCascadeDeleteConvention` convention by removing the `modelBuilder.Conventions.Remove` call we just added.

Taking Control of Model Caching

Throughout this book you have seen how Code First takes care of a lot of things for you, but that you can take control of them and change the behavior when needed. Model caching is no exception; in fact, you likely had no idea that Code First was caching a model for you up to this point. After scanning your classes and applying conventions and configuration, Code First keeps an in-memory version of your model around so that it can be reused in the application instance. This is the reason that the OnModelCreating method is only hit once for each DbContext in an application instance. In this section, you will learn more about what model caching is, when you might need to override the conventions, and how you go about doing that.

Understanding Model Caching

In earlier chapters, you have seen that Code First will automatically discover and build a model based on the DbSet properties that you expose on your context. The model creation process involves taking that set of entity types, running the Code First conventions on them, and then applying any additional configuration that you specified via Data Annotations or the Fluent API. This process isn't cheap on resources and can take some time, especially if your model is large and/or complex. To avoid incurring this cost every time you create an instance of your context, Code First runs this process once and then caches the final model for your context type. Model caching occurs at the AppDomain level.

You can see model caching in action by monitoring when the OnModelCreating method is called on your context. Add a line to the OnModelCreating method that will write to the console whenever it is called:

```
Console.WriteLine("OnModelCreating called!");
```

Modify the Main method to call the InsertDestination method a number of times (Example 7-3). You added the InsertDestination method itself back in Chapter 2.

Example 7-3. Main updated to use the context multiple times

```
static void Main()
{
  Database.SetInitializer(
    new DropCreateDatabaseIfModelChanges<BreakAwayContext>());

  InsertDestination();
  InsertDestination();
  InsertDestination();
}
```

After running the application again, you will see that although the code constructs and uses three separate instances of BreakAwayContext, the OnModelCreating method is only called once. This is because Code First only calls OnModelCreating while creating the model for the first context instance; after that, the final model is cached and is reused for the following uses of BreakAwayContext.

Overriding Default Model Caching

There aren't many situations where you need to take control of model caching. Provided that the model for a given context type stays the same for every instance of that context with an `AppDomain`, the default behavior is going to work as expected. Using the default behavior is also going to give you the best performance, because model creation will only occur one time.

There are some situations where the model for a given context type may vary between instances in the same `AppDomain`. One example would be using a multitenant database. A multitenant database involves having the same model replicated multiple times in the same physical database. For example, you may have a model that is used to store blog posts and a website that displays them. Your website might contain a personal and a work blog that both use the same model. In the database you could have the tables used to store the data for this model replicated in two separate schemas. The tables for your work blog may live in the work schema (`work.Posts`, `work.Comments`, etc.) and the tables for your personal blog might live in the personal schema (`per sonal.Posts`, `personal.Comments`, etc.). Each of these sets of tables is known as a tenant. Database schemas are just one way to distinguish between tenants; there are many other patterns, such as table prefixes.

If your application needs to access multiple tenants from the same `AppDomain`, the mapping between classes and tables is going to be different depending on what tenant you are targeting. Different mapping means a different model, which in turn means the default model caching won't work for you.

Another example would be using the same context to target the same model on different database providers in the same `AppDomain`. Different database providers means different data types for the columns in the database, which in turn means a different model. Let's take a look at this scenario and how to handle model caching.

Add the `TargetMultipleProviders` method shown in Example 7-4. This method uses the same context to access a SQL Server and SQL Server Compact Edition database.

> You will need the SQL Server Compact Edition runtime installed to complete this section. If you have completed Chapter 6, you have already installed the runtime. If not, see "Installing SQL Server Compact Edition" on page 135. You may also remember that in Chapter 6 we had to change our model to target SQL Compact. If you want to test out this code, you will need to make the same change again here. Back in Chapter 3, we configured `Trip.Identifier` to be a database-generated key. Identifier is a GUID property, and SQL Server had no problem generating values for us. SQL Compact, however, isn't able to generate values for GUID columns. If you want to run the application, remove either the Data Annotation or Fluent API call that configures `Trip.Identi fier` as database-generated.

Example 7-4. Reusing a context to target multiple providers

```
static void Main(string[] args)
{
  Database.SetInitializer(new
   DropCreateDatabaseIfModelChanges<BreakAwayContext>());

  TargetMultipleProviders();
}

private static void TargetMultipleProviders()
{
  var sqlString = @"Server=.\SQLEXPRESS;
        Database=DataAccess.BreakAwayContext;
        Trusted_Connection=true";

  using (var connection = new SqlConnection(sqlString))
  {
    using (var context = new BreakAwayContext(connection))
    {
      context.Destinations.Add(new Destination { Name = "Hawaii" });
      context.SaveChanges();
    }
  }

  var sqlCeString =
   @"Data Source=|AppData|\DataAccess.BreakAwayContext.sdf";

  using (var connection = new SqlCeConnection(sqlCeString))
  {
    using (var context = new BreakAwayContext(connection))
    {
      context.Destinations.Add(new Destination { Name = "Hawaii" });
      context.SaveChanges();
    }
  }
}
```

Run the application. You will get an exception when trying to use the context instance that targets SQL Server Compact Edition. This will be a `NotSupportedException` stating that, "Using the same DbCompiledModel to create contexts against different types of database servers is not supported. Instead, create a separate DbCompiledModel for each type of server being used."

To use the same context type with different models in the same AppDomain, you need to externally build a `DbCompiledModel` for each model and then use these to construct the different context instances. `DbContext` exposes a set of constructors that allow you to supply the model to be used, along with connection information. Add a constructor to the `BreakAwayContext` class that allows a `DbCompiledModel` and a `DbConnection` to be supplied:

```
public BreakAwayContext(DbConnection connection,
    DbCompiledModel model)
```

```
    : base(connection, model, contextOwnsConnection: false)
  { }
```

The code in Example 7-5 shows an updated `TargetMultipleProviders` method that
demonstrates how this constructor can now be used to target different database providers, using a different model for each.

Example 7-5. Code updated to work with multiple providers

```
private static void TargetMultipleProviders()
{
  var sql_model = GetBuilder().Build(
    new DbProviderInfo("System.Data.SqlClient", "2008"))
    .Compile();

  var ce_model = GetBuilder().Build(
    new DbProviderInfo("System.Data.SqlServerCe.4.0", "4.0"))
    .Compile();

  var sql_cstr = @"Server=.\SQLEXPRESS;
    Database=DataAccess.BreakAwayContext;
    Trusted_Connection=true";

  using (var connection = new SqlConnection(sql_cstr))
  {
    using (var context =
      new BreakAwayContext(connection, sql_model))
    {
      context.Destinations.Add(new Destination { Name = "Hawaii" });
      context.SaveChanges();
    }
  }

  var ce_cstr =
    @"Data Source=|DataDirectory|\DataAccess.BreakAwayContext.sdf";
  using (var connection = new SqlCeConnection(ce_cstr))
  {
    using (var context = new BreakAwayContext(connection, ce_model))
    {
      context.Database.Initialize(force: true);
      context.Destinations.Add(new Destination { Name = "Hawaii" });
      context.SaveChanges();
    }
  }
}

private static DbModelBuilder GetBuilder()
{
  var builder = new DbModelBuilder();
  builder.Entity<EdmMetadata>().ToTable("EdmMetadata");

  builder.Entity<Activity>();
  builder.Entity<Destination>();
  builder.Entity<Hostel>();
  builder.Entity<InternetSpecial>();
```

```
builder.Entity<Lodging>();
builder.Entity<Person>();
builder.Entity<PersonPhoto>();
builder.Entity<Reservation>();
builder.Entity<Resort>();
builder.Entity<Trip>();

builder.ComplexType<Address>();
builder.ComplexType<Measurement>();
builder.ComplexType<PersonalInfo>();

return builder;
}
```

Let's walk through what the code in the TargetMultipleProviders method is doing. The GetBuilder method is responsible for creating a DbModelBuilder and registering all your classes with the builder. The code in the example registers each class using the DbModelBuilder.Entity and DbModelBuilder.ComplexType methods. This approach will work if you have been using Data Annotations to configure your classes. If you have been using the Fluent API, you should copy the code from your OnModelCreating method to replace this code. Note that you also need to include the EdmMetadata class and map it to the EdmMetadata table; this allows Code First to detect when the model and database go out of sync. When DbContext is responsible for building the model, it will take care of adding this class for you.

The next step is to build and compile the model for the two providers that are going to be targeted. In the example, the invariant name and manifest token for the database provider are supplied to the Build method. As an alternative, there is another overload of Build that accepts a DbConnection to get the provider information from.

With the compiled models created, they can now be used to access the two different databases. Remember that database initialization only occurs once per AppDomain, so only the first database to be used will be initialized automatically. The call to Database.Initialize on the context targeting the second database ensures that the second database is also initialized.

In the end, the new Destination is added to two different databases using the same set of classes and configurations to define duplicate models. Now that we're done using SQL Compact, go ahead and re-enable the configuration to make Trip.Identifier database-generated.

 Remember that building and compiling the model are expensive operations. The resulting compiled model should be cached and reused for all context instances that target the same model.

Working with the EdmMetadata Table

Back in Chapter 2, you learned that, by default, Code First adds an `EdmMetadata` table to your database. There are some advantages in allowing Code First to have this table in the database, but you also have the option of removing it. In this section, you will see how to remove the `EdmMetadata` table from your database. You'll also learn about the implications of removing it.

The `EdmMetadata` table serves a single purpose, and that is to store a snapshot of the model that was used to create the database. Having the snapshot allows Code First to check whether the current model matches the current database or not. The snapshot is stored by taking a SHA256 hash of the database portion of the model. You can see in Figure 7-3 that the `EdmMetadata` table always contains a single row with the hash stored in it.

	Id	ModelHash
1	1	B8D55D4C12B416E071DC41DEB287F61D8C0C3CDD090A87E3...

Figure 7-3. Contents of EdmMetadata table

Coding Against EdmMetadata

Code First uses the `EdmMetadata` table in the included database initializers, but you can also interact with it programmatically using the `EdmMetadata` class in the EntityFramework API. Modify the `Main` method to call a new `UseEdmMetadataTable` method, shown in Example 7-6, to experiment with this class:

Example 7-6. The UseEdmMetadata method

```
static void Main()
{
  Database.SetInitializer(
    new DropCreateDatabaseIfModelChanges<BreakAwayContext>());
  UseEdmMetadataTable();
}

private static void UseEdmMetadataTable()
{
  using (var context = new BreakAwayContext())
  {
    var modelHash = EdmMetadata.TryGetModelHash(context);
    Console.WriteLine("Current Model Hash: {0}", modelHash);

    var databaseHash =
     context.Set<EdmMetadata>().Single().ModelHash;
    Console.WriteLine("Current Database Hash: {0}", databaseHash);

    var compatible =
     context.Database.CompatibleWithModel(throwIfNoMetadata: true);
```

```
    Console.WriteLine("Model Compatible With Database?: {0}",
      compatible);
  }
}
```

This code starts by using the static `EdmMetadata.TryGetModelHash` method to find the hash for the current model. This method will always work for Code First models, but if you attempt to use it with a model created using the designer, it will return null. The `EdmMetadata` class is included as part of your model, so you can use your `DbContext` to interact with it.

The second section of code creates a `DbSet` for the `EdmMetadata` class and then asks for the single row of data so that it can read the hash value from it. Finally, there is a `DbContext.Database.CompatibleWithModel` method that makes it simple to check if the model and database match. This is the method that the database initializers included in the Entity Framework make use of. Specifying `true` for the `throwIfNoMetadata` parameter will cause an exception to be thrown if the `EdmMetadata` table has been excluded from the database. Specifying `false` will cause the method to return `false` if the table is excluded. You can run the code and see that everything currently matches.

Preventing Code First from Creating and Seeking EdmMetadata

The functionality that the `EdmMetadata` table enables is useful, but you may not be happy with Code First adding the extra table to your database. If you don't want Code First to add the `EdmMetadata` table, you can ask it to stop including it. Modify the `BreakAway Context` class to include a line of code that removes the `IncludeMetadataConvention` in the `OnModelCreating` method:

```
    modelBuilder.Conventions.Remove<IncludeMetadataConvention>();
```

So far you have relied on the `DropCreateDatabaseIfModelChanges` initializer to take care of keeping the model and database in sync. However, this initializer relies on the Edm-Metadata table. If you try to run your application, you will get a `NotSupportedExcep tion` stating that

> Model compatibility cannot be checked because the EdmMetadata type was not included in the model. Ensure that IncludeMetadataConvention has been added to the DbMo-delBuilder conventions.

With the `EdmMetadata` table excluded, you can still use the `CreateDatabaseIfNotEx ists` and `DropCreateDatabaseAlways` initializers. If using `CreateDatabaseIfNotExists`, Code First will make no attempt to check that the database and model match and it will simply assume that you have made sure they do. If you make changes to the model, you will also be responsible for making the same changes to the database manually.

Modify the `Main` method to set the `DropCreateDatabaseAlways` initializer and call the `InsertDestination` method you created in Chapter 2 (Example 2-7). Run the application, and you will see that the `EdmMetadata` table is no longer present in your database.

Example 7-7. Main updated to demonstrate EdmMetadata table is removed

```
static void Main()
{
  Database.SetInitializer(
    new DropCreateDatabaseAlways<BreakAwayContext>());
  InsertDestination();
}
```

For our BAGA application, we are perfectly happy for Code First to include the `EdmMe`
`tadata` table in our database. Once you've seen the database without the `EdmMetadata`
table, go ahead and remove the line of configuration you just added to exclude it.
Because Code First just created your database without an `EdmMetadata` table, you'll also
need to go and manually drop the `DataAccess.BreakAwayContext` database from your
localhost\SQLEXPRESS instance. If you don't do this, Code First won't be able to check
compatibility as you change your model in the future.

Using Code First with ObjectContext

Up until now, you have seen Code First being used with the `DbContext` API, which is
the recommended API surface for working with Code First. `DbContext` was introduced
in Entity Framework 4.1 as a lighter-weight and more productive wrapper over the
existing Entity Framework components. The alternative to `DbContext` is the `ObjectCon`
`text` API, and while it is recommended to use `DbContext` with Code First, it is still
possible to use `ObjectContext`. In this chapter, you will see how to build a Code First
model and use it to construct an `ObjectContext`.

DbContext or ObjectContext?

`DbContext` is simply a wrapper over `ObjectContext` and associated classes. If you need
some of the more advanced features that are only available from `ObjectContext`, you
can cast `DbContext` to the `IObjectContextAdapter` interface to access the underlying
`ObjectContext`. This approach allows you to access the functionality from `ObjectCon`
`text` while still being able to write most of your code against the newer `DbContext`. You
might consider using Code First with `ObjectContext` if you have existing applications
that are based on `ObjectContext` and you are swapping from Model First or Database
First to Code First.

Similar to using a `DbContext`-based context, you start by creating a derived context,
except this time it derives from `ObjectContext` and exposes `ObjectSet` properties instead
of `DbSet` properties. Notice in Example 7-8 that when using an `ObjectContext`, you need
to write a bit more code than with the `DbContext`. You must expose a constructor that
accepts an `EntityConnection`. The `ObjectSet` properties also need to be initialized using
the `CreateObjectSet` method; this is something `DbContext` takes care of for you.

Add this new `BreakAwayObjectContext` class to your DataAccess project.

Example 7-8. Implementing ObjectContext

```
using System.Data.EntityClient;
using System.Data.Objects;
using Model;

namespace DataAccess
{
  public class BreakAwayObjectContext : ObjectContext
  {
    public BreakAwayObjectContext(EntityConnection connection)
      : base(connection)
    {
      this.Destinations = this.CreateObjectSet<Destination>();
      this.Lodgings = this.CreateObjectSet<Lodging>();
      this.Trips = this.CreateObjectSet<Trip>();
      this.People = this.CreateObjectSet<Person>();
      this.PersonPhotos = this.CreateObjectSet<PersonPhoto>();
    }

    public ObjectSet<Destination> Destinations { get; private set; }
    public ObjectSet<Lodging> Lodgings { get; private set; }
    public ObjectSet<Trip> Trips { get; private set; }
    public ObjectSet<Person> People { get; private set; }
    public ObjectSet<PersonPhoto> PersonPhotos { get; private set; }
  }
}
```

At this point, `DbContext` would take care of scanning the `DbSet` properties and building a model based on them. But `ObjectContext` has no built-in support for Code First. Code First provides a method to bridge this gap—`DbModelBuilder.UseObjectContext`. In the following walkthrough, you'll learn how to leverage this to create an `ObjectContext` from a Code First model.

Modify the `Main` method to make use of a new `UseObjectContext` method, as shown in Example 7-9.

Example 7-9. Code updated to use BreakAwayObjectContext

```
static void Main()
{
  UseObjectContext();
}

private static void UseObjectContext()
{
  var builder = GetBuilder();

  var cstr = @"Server=.\SQLEXPRESS;
    Database=BreakAwayObjectContext;
    Trusted_Connection=true";
```

```
  using (var connection = new SqlConnection(cstr))
  {
    var model = builder.Build(connection).Compile();
    using (var context =
    model.CreateObjectContext<BreakAwayObjectContext>(connection))
    {
      if (!context.DatabaseExists())
      {
        context.CreateDatabase();
      }
      context.Destinations.AddObject(
      new Destination { Name = "Ayers Rock" });
      context.SaveChanges();
    }
  }
}
```

You start by creating a DbModelBuilder, using the GetBuilder method we added earlier in this chapter. You then use the model builder to create a model and compile it. Note that you must supply the connection or provider information when building the model, as the provider affects the data types, etc. in the resulting model. With the model compiled, you can then use the CreateObjectContext method to construct the ObjectContext. This method relies on the constructor you exposed that accepts a single Entity Connection parameter. ObjectContext doesn't support database initializers, so you also need to write code to check if the database exists and create it if it does not. Note that ObjectContext does not support EdmMetadata either, so there is no way to detect if the model and database are compatible.

Summary

In this chapter, you saw a variety of advanced features that Code First provides. These features are provided to make sure that you can override what Code First does by default in situations where the default behavior just doesn't work for your scenario. Most applications won't require you to use these features, but it's good to have an understanding of what is available in case you ever need them.

We've now covered Code First from top to bottom. We started with a high-level overview of what Code First is. You then learned how Code First builds the model and how you can customize the model by using configuration. You saw how to influence which database Code First connects to and how that database is initialized. And finally in this chapter, we wrapped things up with some advanced topics.

The final chapter of this book will help prepare you for what's coming in future releases of Code First.

CHAPTER 8

What's Coming Next for Code First

So far, this book has covered all of the Code First components that reached their final release at the time of writing. There are, however, some notable features that are still in preview at this time that you should be aware of. You'll gain the ability to migrate a database schema as your Code First model evolves, reverse engineer a Code First model from an existing database, and many other useful tasks.

These features are available as add-ons to the EntityFramework NuGet package and can be downloaded separately. Currently there are two add-ons available. The first, the `EntityFramework.Migrations` NuGet package, adds database migration capabilities to Code First. The second, Entity Framework Power Tools, provides some extra design time tooling for working with Code First and is available on Visual Studio Gallery.

Code First Migrations

Throughout this book we have used database initializers to drop and recreate the database every time the model changes. This is far from ideal, because in doing so, you lose any data every time the model changes. That might be acceptable while you're developing locally, but it's definitely not a viable solution once you want to push changes into production! Currently you are forced to use a schema compare tool or a hand-written script to push database changes to the production database.

Since Code First was released, one of the most common requests from the developer community was for a migrations solution. Migrations allow you to incrementally evolve your database schema as your model changes. There are many migration solutions available, but none that are integrated with Code First. Most of these solutions take a similar approach to providing database migration functionality. Each set of changes to the database is expressed in a code file, known as a migration. The migrations are ordered, typically using a timestamp, and a table in the database keeps track of which migrations have been applied to the database.

The Entity Framework team has been working on providing a migrations solution that is tightly integrated with Code First. Code First Migrations Alpha 3 became available in early September 2011. Details on the Alpha 3 release of Code First Migrations can be found at *http://blogs.msdn.com/b/adonet/archive/2011/09/21/code-first-migrations -alpha-3-released.aspx*. This early preview is focused on the developer experience inside Visual Studio and allows migrations to be created and executed against the database as your Code First model is changed.

Code First Migrations is available as the `EntityFramework.Migrations` NuGet package. Once installed, it adds a couple of commands to the Package Manager Console that can be used to generate and run migrations.

As you make changes to your Code First model, you can ask Code First Migrations to create a migration that will apply the corresponding changes to the database. Migrations are expressed in code, and once a migration has been created, you are free to edit the code that was generated for you. Example 8-1 shows what a migration can look like.

Example 8-1. Sample migration

```
namespace BreakAway.Migrations
{
    using System.Data.Entity.Migrations;

    public partial class SampleChanges : DbMigration
    {
        public override void Up()
        {
            AddColumn(
                "Destinations",
                "Description",
                c => c.String());

            ChangeColumn(
                "Destinations",
                "Name",
                c => c.String(maxLength: 100));
        }

        public override void Down()
        {
            ChangeColumn(
                "Destinations",
                "Name",
                c => c.String());

            DropColumn(
                "Destinations",
                "Description");
        }
    }
}
```

The migrations are expressed using an API that is similar to the Fluent API you've been using to configure the model. In the example, you can see that a `Description` column is being added to the `Destinations` table and the `Name` column is having its maximum length changed to 50. A provider model is used to translate the operations defined in code into database specific SQL.

Code First Migrations also supports *automatic migrations*, which allow simple changes, such as column additions, to be performed without having a migration present in your project. You can use automatic migrations and code-based migrations in the same solution to allow the correct level of control for each change you make.

Entity Framework Power Tools

The first Entity Framework Power Tools Community Technical Preview (CTP 1) was made available in May 2011. This package can be installed through the Visual Studio Extension Manager or downloaded directly from the Visual Studio Gallery at *http:// visualstudiogallery.msdn.microsoft.com/72a60b14-1581-4b9b-89f2-846072eff19d*. Once installed, the Power Tools add designer tools to Visual Studio that can be accessed through context menus in the Visual Studio Solution Explorer.

Reverse Engineer Code First

With this designer tool installed, you'll find a new menu option—Entity Framework— on the project context menu in Solution Explorer (Figure 8-1). The new item has a submenu item called "Reverse Engineer Code First." Selecting this option will prompt you to point to an existing database that you would like to map classes to using Code First. The tool will use the schema of the database to generate a Code First context, a set of POCO classes, and a set of configuration classes to map the POCO classes to the database. You can see what these classes look like in the blog post Quick Look at Reverse Engineer DB into Code First Classes (*http://thedatafarm.com/blog/data-access/ quick-look-at-reverse-engineer-db-into-code-first-classes*).

The reverse engineer process is designed to be a one-time code generation to get you started against an existing database. Once the code is generated, you may need to tweak it to match your exact database schema. For example, CTP1 does not generate the correct mapping code for tables that are not in the dbo schema. If you have tables in another schema, you would need to edit the ToTable call in the relevant configuration objects to specify the correct schema.

 CTP1 of the Power Tools only supports reverse engineering to C#. The Entity Framework team will introduce VB.NET capabilities in a future release.

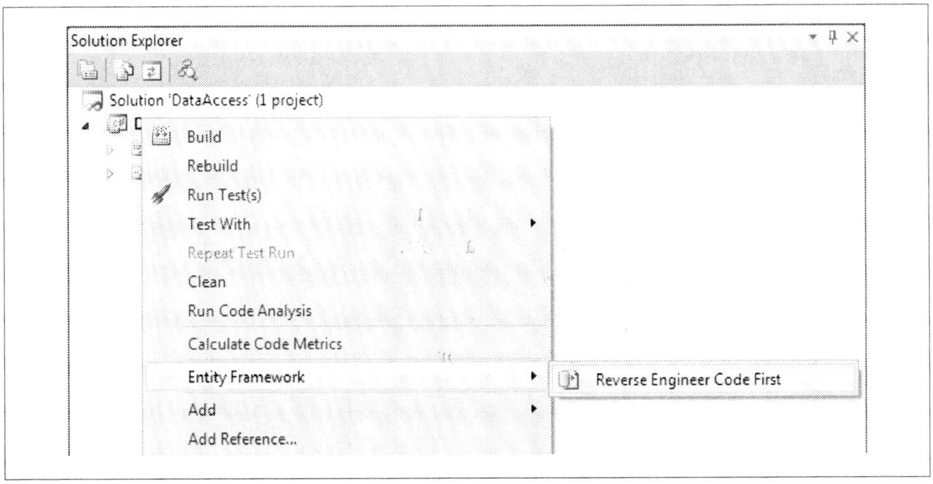

Figure 8-1. Project context menu

Viewing a Code First Model

The Entity Framework Power Tools also adds an Entity Framework item to the context menu for classes that inherit from DbContext (Figure 8-2). When you right-click the code file in Solution Explorer, this Entity Framework entry has four options. The first three provide you different views of the model for the selected context.

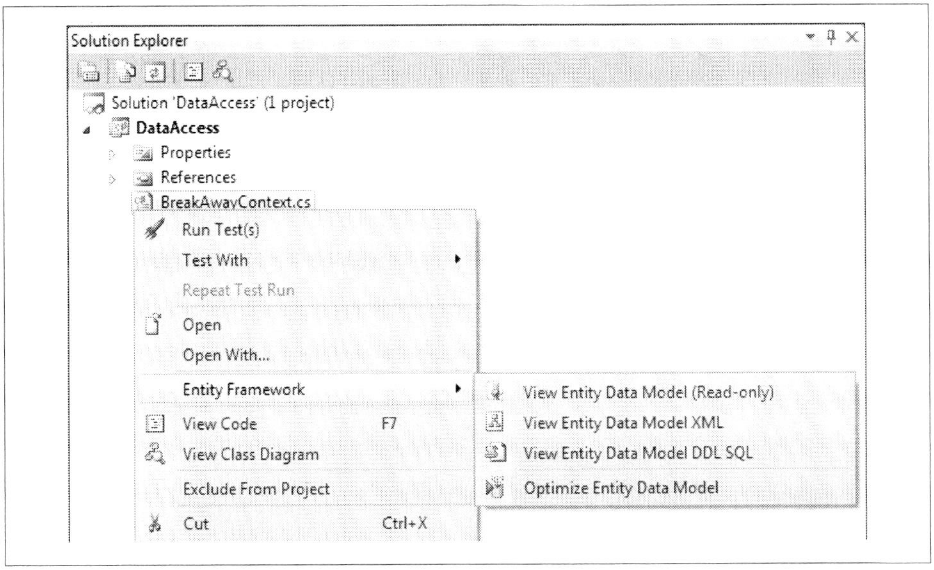

Figure 8-2. Code First context menu

View Entity Data Model (Read-only)

The "View Entity Data Model (Read-only)" option will launch the Entity Data Model designer and display the model defined by the context. The Power Tools achieve this by writing out a temporary EDMX file that represents the model and opening it with the designer.

This is a read-only view of the model, and any changes you make will not result in changes being made to your code. You are only able to make changes because the designer, which ships as part of Visual Studio, does not have a read-only mode.

The ability to view the model can be useful if you are trying to work out how Code First is interpreting your classes and configuration. The designer also displays mapping so you can see how Code First is mapping your classes and properties to columns and tables in the database.

View Entity Data Model XML

The "View Entity Data Model XML" option will load up the EDMX equivalent of your Code First model in the XML editor.

This option is primarily used by the Entity Framework team to identify issues in the model that is being generated by Code First.

View Entity Data Model DDL SQL

The *View Entity Data Model DDL SQL* option allows you to generate the same SQL script that Code First would use to generate a database from your model. This can be useful if you have been developing with Code First and now need to hand a SQL script off to your DBA to create a production database.

Optimize Entity Data Model

The fourth option in the Entity Framework menu item that's attached to the context class is "Optimize Entity Data Model." This allows you to perform *view generation* on your Code First model.

View generation is a process that Entity Framework performs to calculate the SQL statements that will be used to Select, Insert, Update, and Delete for each type in your model. This process typically occurs the first time you use your context within an application process. If you have a large and/or complex model, view generation can be an expensive operation, taking several minutes or even hours in very large models.

To avoid incurring this cost every time your application runs, you can use Pre-Compiled Views. That's exactly what this option does: it precalculates the SQL and stores it in a code file in your project. Entity Framework will pick up this code at runtime and use the precalculated views rather than performing View generation. If you change your model after performing view generation, you will need to rerun this option to calculate the views again.

Pre-Compiled Views are a fairly advanced feature, and it is not recommended that you use them unless you hit a performance issue related to View Generation.

Pre-compilation and view generation are not unique to Code First. These features have been available for EDMX files since the first version of Entity Framework. The Power Tools simply let you also take advantage of these features when using Code First. You can read more about precompiled views and view generation in Chapter 20 of *Programming Entity Framework*, second edition.

Following the Entity Framework Team

There are a number of ways you can keep up to date on new features that the Entity Framework team is developing—and even influence what features they work on next. The ADO.NET Team Blog (*http://blogs.msdn.com/adonet*) is used by the EF team to share announcements about new and upcoming releases. The EF team also has an EF Design Blog (*http://blogs.msdn.com/efdesign*), where they share early thinking about new features they are about to start working on. This allows you to have input into the design of features before they are implemented and end up in a preview. Finally, the EF team has a user voice site (*http://ef.mswish.net*) where you can add and vote on feature requests.

About the Authors

Julia Lerman is the leading independent authority on the Entity Framework and has been using and teaching the technology since its inception in 2006. She is well known in the .NET community as a Microsoft MVP, ASPInsider, and INETA Speaker. Julia is a frequent presenter at technical conferences around the world and writes articles for many well-known technical publications, including the "Data Points" column in *MSDN Magazine*. Julia lives in Vermont with her husband, Rich, and gigantic dog, Sampson, where she runs the Vermont.NET User Group. You can read her blog at *www.thedatafarm.com/blog* and follow her on Twitter at julielerman.

Rowan Miller is based in Seattle, Washington, and works as a Program Manager for the ADO.NET Entity Framework team at Microsoft. Prior to moving to the United States, he resided in the small state of Tasmania in Australia. Rowan speaks at technical conferences and blogs at *http://romiller.com*. Outside of technology, Rowan's passions include snowboarding, mountain biking, horse riding, rock climbing, and pretty much anything else that involves being active. The primary focus of his life, however, is to follow Jesus.

Get even more for your money.

Join the O'Reilly Community, and register the O'Reilly books you own. It's free, and you'll get:

- $4.99 ebook upgrade offer
- 40% upgrade offer on O'Reilly print books
- Membership discounts on books and events
- Free lifetime updates to ebooks and videos
- Multiple ebook formats, DRM FREE
- Participation in the O'Reilly community
- Newsletters
- Account management
- 100% Satisfaction Guarantee

Signing up is easy:

1. **Go to: oreilly.com/go/register**
2. **Create an O'Reilly login.**
3. **Provide your address.**
4. **Register your books.**

Note: English-language books only

To order books online:

oreilly.com/store

For questions about products or an order:

orders@oreilly.com

To sign up to get topic-specific email announcements and/or news about upcoming books, conferences, special offers, and new technologies:

elists@oreilly.com

For technical questions about book content:

booktech@oreilly.com

To submit new book proposals to our editors:

proposals@oreilly.com

O'Reilly books are available in multiple DRM-free ebook formats. For more information:

oreilly.com/ebooks

O'REILLY®

Spreading the knowledge of innovators | oreilly.com

The information you need, when and where you need it.

With Safari Books Online, you can:

Access the contents of thousands of technology and business books

- Quickly search over 7000 books and certification guides
- Download whole books or chapters in PDF format, at no extra cost, to print or read on the go
- Copy and paste code
- Save up to 35% on O'Reilly print books
- **New!** Access mobile-friendly books directly from cell phones and mobile devices

Stay up-to-date on emerging topics before the books are published

- Get on-demand access to evolving manuscripts.
- Interact directly with authors of upcoming books

Explore thousands of hours of video on technology and design topics

- Learn from expert video tutorials
- Watch and replay recorded conference sessions

CPSIA information can be obtained at www.ICGtesting.com
Printed in the USA
BVOW061630301012

304244BV00002B/35/P